THROUGH THE LENS:
CAPTURING LIFE'S ESSENCE

A JOURNEY INTO THE ART AND SCIENCE,
DIGITAL OF PHOTOGRAPHY

BY

BERNARD

TABLE OF CONTENTS

PRESENTATION

Hey there, fellow shutterbugs!

Welcome to a transformative journey through the lens of imagination and creativity! If you're holding this book right now, you're about to embark on an exciting adventure into the soul of photography — a world where pixels and emotions dance in perfect harmony. This isn't just another photography manual; it's an invitation to explore your artistry and discover the stories waiting to be told through your camera. Why did I write this? Well, I'm a passionate photographer who believes that the essence of photography goes beyond mere technical skills. It's about connection, emotion, and empathy. I wanted this book to serve as a bridge, connecting aspiring photographers with the deeper, richer narrative that lies at the heart of every image. Throughout my years of capturing fleeting moments, I found that the most poignant photographs are born from genuine connections between the photographer and the subject. And that pivotal realization became the driving force behind this book.

As you flip through these pages, expect to dive into thematic chapters that explore a wealth of topics, from the historical evolution of photography to practical exercises that ignite your creativity. Each chapter is woven with personal anecdotes that reflect my journey, sprinkled with insights gleaned from mentors whose wisdom shaped my perspective. It's like sitting down with an old friend over a cup of coffee, sharing stories and sparking new ideas. There's a rich tapestry of knowledge embedded in each chapter — whether it's honing your technical skills, understanding the dance of light, or learning how to create compelling compositions. This book aims to educate and inspire, encouraging you to approach photography with fresh eyes and a renewed sense of curiosity.

Imagine diving into 'The Soul of Photography,' where you'll explore your own emotional connection to your subjects. Or in 'Composition: The Art of Arrangement,' you'll find yourself experimenting with the rule of thirds and leading lines — trust me, these techniques will elevate your photographs to new heights! And just when you think you've got it all figured out, we'll flip the script in 'The Digital Revolution,' where we'll demystify digital technology and its impact on your artistic expression.

But wait — there's more! Are you ready for hands-on challenges? Chapter after chapter, you'll find practical exercises designed to push your creative boundaries and to encourage a playful exploration of photography. I firmly believe that creativity thrives in an environment of experimentation, and I'll make sure to light that spark! Whether you're a newbie or an experienced photographer seeking to break through creative blocks, there's something in these pages for you.

Now, you may ask: what makes a photograph powerful? The answer lies in storytelling. It's a facet we'll delve into deeply, giving you the tools and inspiration to capture not only moments but also the feelings they evoke. From 'Emotion in Every Frame' to 'Telling Stories Through Series,' you'll learn to weave narratives that resonate with viewers long after they've put your photo down. In the end, we'll take a step back to reflect on your progression and envision your future path in 'Reflections: Your Photographic Journey.' It's vital that you celebrate how far you've come and set intentions for what's next!

So, what are you waiting for? Grab your camera, open your mind, and let's embark on this creative quest together! Each chapter is geared to draw you in and provoke your thoughts, turning the mundane into the extraordinary through the art of photography.

I'm thrilled to have you on this journey, and I can't wait for you to experience all the magic that lies ahead. Ready to take the plunge? Let's go!

With inspiration and excitement,

Bernard

CHAPTER 1

THE SOUL OF PHOTOGRAPHY

The Emotional Connection

As photographers, we often find ourselves standing behind our cameras, poised to capture a fleeting moment. But what makes a photograph resonate? What elevates a simple image into something profound and emotional? It is the connection we establish with our subjects, and the empathy we cultivate during the process of creation. This subchapter dives deep into what it means to connect with your subject, exploring the intricate web of emotions that can transform a photograph from a mere depiction to a powerful narrative.

Every photograph tells a story. The trick is uncovering the layers beneath the surface, revealing the essence of the moment. Whether we're navigating the bustling streets of a vibrant city or sitting face-to-face with a child, we must learn to delve into the emotional foundation of those we photograph. By understanding their feelings, fears, hopes, and dreams, we elevate our photography beyond the technical aspects and infuse it with humanity.

Imagine walking through a market filled with vibrant colors and bustling energy. The sounds of laughter and the aroma of spices fill the air. You see a vendor selling fragrant flowers, their hands delicately arranging blooms to create stunning bouquets. In that brief moment, you instinctively feel a connection to this vendor. You sense the passion they pour into their work, the pride of nurturing life through each petal. It is this visceral understanding that transforms your photograph. You raise your camera, but before you capture the moment, you engage with the vendor.

"Your flowers are beautiful; how long have you been doing this?" you ask.

The vendor, surprised by your inquiry, takes a moment to gather their thoughts. They smile, a warmth radiating from their eyes. "I've been doing this for over twenty years. It's my family tradition. My mother taught me everything I know."

As they speak, you notice how their expression shifts. The initial surprise gives way to nostalgia, pride, and joy. With every word, you capture not only their image but their essence—an emotional portrait that tells a story of legacy, commitment, and love for their craft.

Before clicking the shutter, you have painted the canvas of your photograph with rich emotional hues. The raw emotion you've identified is captured alongside the colors and shapes of the flowers, transforming an ordinary moment into an extraordinary tale.

In street photography, connections are often ephemeral. The encounter is fleeting, yet the emotions can linger. Such moments require us to be alert, sensitive, and receptive. Empathy does not always mean lengthy conversations; sometimes, it is the silent observance of the emotions written on someone's face that speaks volumes.

Consider another scenario: a candid shot of an elderly man sitting on a park bench. His eyes are weary, and a hint of melancholy graces his features. Instead of merely snapping the picture from a distance, you take a moment to sit next to him on the bench. Your presence is unassuming, non-intrusive. You sit in silence, observing the world around you—the fluttering leaves, the laughter of children, the rhythm of life.

As the sun dips below the horizon, you turn to him and say, "It's a beautiful evening, isn't it?"

He nods, a small smile breaking through the fog of his sorrow. You share in that moment of vulnerability, and he begins to share fragments of his past—memories of love, loss, and a lifetime of experiences. As he recounts his story, you notice the way his eyes light up when he speaks of his late wife. Those fleeting details evoke emotions that are palpable, almost tangible.

Now, when you click the shutter, you are not just capturing an old man on a bench; you are capturing a life filled with love, longing, and memories. The image resonates, allowing viewers to sense the emotional depth of the moment without needing to know the man's story; it's in the gaze, the smile, and the way he holds the weight of his history in his expression.

Understanding the complexities of our subjects is pivotal, whether they are strangers on the street or loved ones posing for a portrait. In the world of portrait photography, the interaction can be more intentional. Portrait sessions often involve communication and trust-building, allowing for a deeper connection between the photographer and the subject.

When I photograph children, I find myself crouching down to their eye level, a tangible act of empathy. It helps bridge the gap of age and experience, and suddenly, I see the world as they do—full of wonder and innocence. My camera becomes a vessel of storytelling, one that reflects not just their image but their emotions and spontaneity. All it takes is a gentle request to laugh, a silly face, or an invitation to share their thoughts. The resulting images, bursting with life, convey joy and authenticity.

In one of my favorite portrait sessions, I had the pleasure of photographing a young girl who loved to dance. As we chatted about her dreams and aspirations, I discovered the passion that ignited her spirit. I asked her to show me her favorite dance move, and the transformation was immediate. The timid child melted away, replaced by a confident performer radiating joy.

As the rhythmic music played, I clicked the shutter in a flurry of frames, capturing not just her movements but the sheer exuberance of her spirit. The profound connection we had established allowed me to document her in the most honest form, each photograph alive with the rhythm of her heart.

Often, the power of empathy can be amplified further when we venture into the lives of communities and cultures vastly different from our own. Engaging with the stories of people from various backgrounds opens up new vistas of connection. The act of listening to their experiences and understanding their struggles adds layers to our photographs.

On one occasion, I participated in a project aimed at highlighting the lives of refugees. I met a woman who had fled her war-torn country, leaving everything behind. As she shared her journey—filled with trials and the hope of better days—my heart ached for her struggles. Every detail painted a vivid picture of resilience, love, and loss.

Interacting with her required sensitivity and patience. I sat with her in her modest apartment, simply listening. There were no elaborate setups or strict poses; it was about capturing the subtlety of her experience. As we spoke, I felt a connection growing—one built on genuine human emotion.

In that moment, I raised my camera, capturing the glint of determination in her eyes. The soft light pouring through the window accentuated the wisdom etched into her features. Suddenly, the image was no longer just of a refugee; it represented stories of bravery and strength. We must remember that behind every face lies a history, an experience that shaped who they are today.

Returning to the digital realm, we often forget the importance of connecting to our subjects beyond the lens. In the age of social media, where interactions can often feel fleeting or transactional, it's crucial to strive for meaningful connections. Authenticity can shine through imagery, creating a bridge between the viewer and the subject.

When I post images of my work online, I make it a point to share the stories behind the photographs. I invite viewers into the journey— allowing them to step into the moments I captured. By doing so, I foster empathy and connection not just between myself and my subjects, but also between the viewer and the story that unfolds.

For photographers, the quest is not merely about documentation; it is about storytelling. As storytellers, we must explore our subjects' feelings, their narratives, and transform that understanding into the images we create. The world is filled with individuals whose stories deserve to be shared—a tapestry of experiences, emotions, and connections that are waiting to be captured.

Understanding our subjects leads us to contemplate our own feelings as photographers. What emotions drive us when we take a photograph? Are we capturing joy, sorrow, love, or hope? Reflecting on our emotions allows us to connect more profoundly with our subjects. When we embrace vulnerability and openness, we create space for our subjects to be seen and heard.

Consider this: the next time you pick up your camera, take a moment to breathe. Before you click, pause and reflect. Wander through empathy, understanding what you hope to capture—not just the image before you, but the emotional resonance behind it. Engage with your subjects, share their experiences, and allow those emotions to flow through your lens.

As you strive to connect with each person you photograph, remember that these moments, filled with emotions, stories, and life experiences, are the threads that weave the fabric of your photography. They will not only enhance the impact of your art but will also nurture your growth as a creative storyteller.

Every face has a story. Every moment deserves to be cherished. Each photograph can echo an emotional connection. As you embark on your journey behind the lens, cultivate and nurture those connections, for they hold the power to elevate your work into a realm where photography becomes an enduring narrative—one that transcends the boundaries of time and resonates with those who gaze upon it. Through empathy, you can transform an ordinary frame into an extraordinary testament of life's beautiful tapestry.

Empathy as a Tool

Empathy is often thought of as an emotional skill, but in the realm of photography, it transforms not only the photographer's approach but also the nature of the images captured. It acts as a bridge between the photographer and their subject, allowing for genuine connection and understanding. Empathy, in this context, isn't just about feeling for someone; it's about feeling with someone, immersing oneself in their experience, and communicating that sentiment through the lens.

In my early days as a photographer, I often approached subjects with a sense of detachment, treating them like objects to be documented rather than individuals with their own stories. I recall a particular experience during a street photography workshop in a bustling city. There I was, camera in hand, bustling through crowds, capturing the energy of urban life, but something felt amiss. I was documenting moments, yet lacking the depth I craved. This changed dramatically when I decided to pause and truly observe a small gathering at a corner café.

As I sat on a nearby bench, I noticed a group of elderly men animatedly chatting. Instead of aiming my camera at them, I listened to their laughter, watched their gestures, and absorbed the warmth of their camaraderie. My focus shifted from simply taking a photograph to capturing a moment steeped in joy and connection. When I eventually raised my camera, I found that the images reflected not just their faces but their vitality, their shared memories, and the moments that defined their friendship.

By immersing myself in their world—listening to their stories, witnessing their interactions—I could feel a connection that was palpable. The resulting photographs, now infused with emotion and narrative, transformed what could have been mere snapshots into evocative pieces of art that resonated with viewers. This experience taught me that the cultivation of empathy is a critical tool for every photographer, allowing us to capture not only what our eyes see but also what our hearts feel.

Empathy can be developed in various ways. One essential technique is active listening. This doesn't simply mean hearing the words that someone says; it requires engaging fully in the conversation. It entails asking questions, reflecting on what is shared, and responding thoughtfully. As photographers, this skill becomes incredibly important when we are in the presence of our subjects.

For instance, during a portrait session, asking open-ended questions can encourage subjects to share their stories and emotions. "What's been on your mind lately?" or "Can you tell me about a significant moment in your life?" These questions invite more profound conversation and, in return, allow us to capture raw, authentic emotions. The expressions that emerge from such dialogues can bring a depth to our images that a simple "Say cheese!" never could.

I remember one particular portrait session with a young woman named Leila, who had recently lost her father. Initially, she was shy and reluctant to open up. Instead of setting up my camera and firing away, I took a step back. I invited her to share stories about her father, asking her to speak about her fondest memories. As she spoke, layers of emotion surfaced; I saw the weight of her loss in her eyes. It was then that she seemed to let her guard down, allowing vulnerability to seep into her expressions. The resulting photographs reflected her journey through grief, capturing not just a moment but an entire narrative—a testament to the power of empathy.

Another vital tool in the empathy toolkit is observing body language. Our subjects communicate a wealth of information through gestures, posture, and facial expressions. Becoming attuned to these non-verbal cues can help us understand them better and allow us to seize the right moments to capture. This understanding can elevate our photography, adding layers of meaning that might otherwise be overlooked.

Consider the difference between photographing someone smiling directly at the camera versus capturing a candid moment where they are lost in thought or in laughter with a friend. The former may produce a technically pleasing image, but the latter resonates with authenticity and emotion. During one memorable shoot at a family reunion, I witnessed a grandmother gaze fondly at her grandchildren, a soft smile gracing her lips as she recalled cherished moments.

Capturing that fleeting gaze and the tenderness reflected in her eyes told a much richer story than a posed family portrait ever could. That one frame summarized years of love, memories, and connection.

To foster the growth of these empathetic skills, I suggest engaging in practical exercises that encourage you to step outside your comfort zone. The following activities can aid in honing your ability to connect deeply with your subjects and enhance your craft overall:

1. **Active Listening Practice**: Pair up with a friend and take turns sharing a personal story. As each person speaks, the listener should aim to ask follow-up questions that delve deeper into the narrative. Afterward, discuss how empathetic listening impacted the conversation's depth and how it may translate into future photography sessions.

2. **Body Language Observation Walk**: Spend an afternoon in a public space, such as a park or café, observing the body language of individuals or groups. Take notes on how people interact—the smiles, gestures, or postures that convey various emotions. This will cultivate your ability to read non-verbal cues when you interact with your subjects.

3. **Emotion-Focused Portrait Challenge**: Select a subject, either someone you know well or a willing stranger, and propose an outdoor portrait session centered on capturing a specific emotion. Before shooting, discuss the chosen emotion with them. For example, if the focus is on happiness, ask them to reflect on what brings them joy. During the shoot, provide prompts that encourage genuine expressions reflective of that emotion. Review the resulting images and evaluate their authenticity.

4. **Documentary Impulse**: Select a theme that resonates with you—joy, isolation, community—and document moments related to that theme over a week. Aim to interact with your subjects and engage in conversations while capturing candid

moments. Reflect on how the depth of those interactions influenced the images you created.

These exercises not only foster empathy but also encourage reflection on your photographic intentions. The process of connecting with subjects is not just about creating captivating images; it is about enriching the visual narrative that emerges. Envision a project where you capture people engaging in their passions—musicians performing, chefs at work, or artists creating. The heartbeat of that project will lie in the connections you nurture, the stories you unearth, and the emotions you bring forth through your lens.

As you practice these skills, consider the emotions you wish to convey in your work. Photography has the incredible power to communicate feelings without words. This connection between the feelings captured in a photograph and the emotions that resonate with an audience is what elevates photography from mere documentation to art.

Reflect on this: When you pause and connect with your subjects, what stories do you want your images to tell? What emotions do you want your viewers to feel? Intimacy and authenticity shine through photographs that resonate with the emotional fabric of experiences.

Empathy has the power to transform mundane moments into extraordinary narratives. Take a moment to consider the photographs you find most moving. What makes them resonate? More often than not, it is the emotion captured within them, whether it's joy, sorrow, or nostalgia, that holds an audience's gaze.

As you embark on your journey, invite empathy to be a guiding principle in your work. Let it fuel your curiosity and deepen your connections. Allow yourself to be moved by the stories surrounding you, and endeavor to translate that emotional richness into your photography. Through moments of genuine connection, the images you create will intrigue, provoke thought, and—most importantly— connect with the human experience.

The beauty of our craft lies not only in the pixels and settings of our cameras but in the spirit of the connections we build and the stories we tell. Each frame is an opportunity to bridge the divide between photographer and subject, to elevate the act of seeing into a dance of understanding. Embrace empathy as your tool, and witness how it transforms not just how you photograph, but how you see the world around you. Remember that capturing authentic moments isn't solely about technique—it's about heart, connection, and the desire to share the essence of life through your unique lens.

Creating Authentic Moments

The art of photography transcends simple technical execution; it is an intricate dance between emotion and technical prowess. When aiming to create authentic moments, one must cultivate both skills. Authenticity, in this context, refers to the genuine expressions and interactions of a subject that resonate on an emotional level, creating a bond between the viewer and the photograph.

Patience is often overlooked in the fast-paced world we inhabit today, where quick clicks and instant gratification reign supreme. Yet, in photography, it can be the key ingredient that unlocks extraordinary moments. The most compelling images don't always occur spontaneously; they sometimes require extended time spent with one's subjects or in one's environment. This subchapter seeks to illuminate those crucial qualities that help photographers embrace patience and timing, allowing them to document life's authentic moments.

Consider a story from my early days photographing street life in a vibrant urban neighborhood. It was a sunny Saturday afternoon filled with bustling energy, yet the atmosphere felt electric. As I strolled along the vibrant streets, I stumbled across a street performer—a man playing soulful jazz on a saxophone. The crowd gathered, captivated, and I felt an undeniable urge to capture the scene. However, in my eagerness, I snapped a few photos and moved along. While the images were technically sound, they lacked the intensity and emotion I soon realized existed in that moment.

I decided to return, taking a step back to soak in the scene. I positioned myself at a distance, allowing the music to wash over me and the emotions of the onlookers to unfold. I observed as families laughed, friends swayed, and strangers closed their eyes, lost in the melodies. Here, I learned that the act of waiting—of becoming part of the energy flowing through the crowd—allowed me to blend in rather than intrude. After a while, I felt the authenticity of the moment rising to the surface. It was during that pause, that stillness, that I managed to capture the culminating frame—a child dancing, captured mid-jump with joy, her small hands raised toward the sky as if reaching for the music itself.

That image was more than just a photograph; it encapsulated a spirit of spontaneity that occurred because I practiced patience. This moment of joyful dance was a fleeting instance, but it resonated profoundly, showcasing the unfiltered emotion in its purest form. If I had rushed to take my initial shots and left, dismissing the need to absorb the scene, I would have forfeited the excitement of that moment.

Through such experiences, I became acutely aware that patience holds resonance in all sorts of photography, not just street scenes. When I gravitated toward portrait photography, this lesson echoed even louder. Engaging with subjects often means entering an intricate relationship built on trust, vulnerability, and authenticity. A candid portrait requires more than a well-timed shutter; it requires an understanding of the nuances of human connection.

As I began working with a middle-aged woman from my community who had spent decades caring for others, my initial attempts to photograph her were met with trepidation. She shifted uncomfortably, presenting a stilted demeanor that betrayed her unease. The tension in the air felt palpable; it was clear that the moment wasn't right. Instead of pushing through, I paused, engaging her in conversation about her passions, her struggles, and her dreams.

Over the course of our dialogue—our authentic moments together—I learned about her love for gardening and how it grounded her amid life's storms. Armed with this understanding, I chose a setting in her garden, surrounded by vibrant blooms and the warmth of sunlight filtering through leaves. With each click of the shutter, I felt the dynamic between us evolve. Instead of snatching pictures of an anxious subject, I captured moments filled with tranquility as she shared snippets of her life. I could see her laughter, vulnerability, and strength shine through in each frame. Authenticity blossomed when she was allowed to lower her guard, revealing layers of emotion and depth.

Through these encounters, I realized that being present during the process of capturing photography is crucial to creating authentic moments. Authenticity does not materialize from behind a lens alone; it emerges from the shared emotional experiences and mutual respect between the subject and photographer. This is not a mere technique—it is an approach that transforms your style to tell a compelling narrative.

Now, let's delve deeper into the practical considerations for creating authentic moments. First and foremost, consider your intent. What emotions or stories do you wish to capture? When you approach a scene with clear motivations, it guides your interaction with both your environment and the subjects within it. Create a grounded plan, but remain flexible, ready to adapt as the moment unfolds.

Practical exercises can help you cultivate these abilities. Here are several techniques to immerse yourself in the process of documenting life authentically:

1. **Time Yourself**: Begin your photography session by setting aside a designated time, such as an hour, to solely observe your surroundings without any camera present. Note the colors, movements, sounds, and rhythms around you. Maintain a journal of thoughts, ideas, or sketches of potential frames. This exercise raises awareness of your shooting environment, encourages observation, and brings forth inspiration before picking up your camera.

2. **Establish Rapport**: If you're entering a portrait session, spend time connecting with your subjects. Engage them in conversation, ask questions, and listen to their stories. Build trust to allow them to reveal their authentic selves. Even simple daily interactions, such as asking a stranger some questions on the street, can be great practice for building rapport.

3. **Immerse Yourself in Communities**: Attend local events or engage with diverse communities, focusing on capturing the essence of their lives. Take time to walk through neighborhoods, markets, or festivities. Uncover stories that often get overlooked, allowing serendipitous moments to guide your lens rather than simply seeking familiar subjects.

4. **Set Up "Waiting" Stations**: Identifying optimal spots in your environment to photograph can create opportunities to observe actions and interactions that reflect authenticity. Select café corners, park benches, or community gathering spaces. Settle into these waiting stations with your camera prepared. By observing from a distance, you might catch discrete glances, genuine laughter, or spontaneous acts that might not have occurred had you intruded too early.

5. **Embrace Movement**: Cultivate a sense of dynamic engagement by photographing subjects in motion. Life is full of action, whether at sporting events, dance performances, or bustling markets. Most often, the most authentic emotions emerge when people are engrossed in doing what they love. Capture the essence of life in motion rather than waiting for the posed shot.

6. **Practice Storytelling**: Choose a specific theme and document everyday life revolving around it. Whether it's capturing joy, solitude, tradition, or culture, practice building a cohesive body of work around a singular narrative. Reflect on how images interact with one another to create a visual story.

7. **Review & Reflect**: After each photographic session, take time to review your work thoughtfully. Identify which shots resonate with authenticity and reflect on why that is. Ask yourself what elements led to the creation of those moments, what emotions they evoke, and how you can replicate this next time.

Through these exercises, the aim isn't to replicate someone else's authentic moments but rather to cultivate your visual storytelling voice. Photography is inherently subjective; our perspectives color every image we take. It's essential to refine our techniques while nurturing the emotional quality of our compositions. When we weave in patience and timing, we invest essence and soul into our photography.

As this journey unfolds, the symbiotic relationship between photographer and subject evolves. Viewers often engage with imagery that feels more than just visually pleasant; they seek connection, narratives that evoke emotion, and experiences that resonate on a deeper level.

Authenticity may seem elusive at times, but it exists in the unscripted moments of life—waiting to be captured when we take the time to show up, engage, and listen. The heart of photography thrives on vulnerability, whether it's from our subjects or from our openness to experience life through our lens. In doing so, we not only capture beautiful images but also forge deeper connections to the world around us.

In conclusion, as we pursue authenticity in our work, let us remember that our lens is merely an extension of our consciousness. The stories we capture and the moments we immortalize reveal not just the surface of the world but invite viewers to engage with the essence of humanity and the beauty that resides in each fleeting instant. Embrace the patience, practice the art of observation, and immerse yourself in your subjects' stories, and your photography will illuminate the authentic moments that dwell in the heart of life itself.

CHAPTER 2

THE EVOLUTION OF THE LENS

From Pinhole to Digital

The origins of photography can be traced back to the camera obscura, a simple yet fascinating optical phenomenon that dates back to ancient times. It was a device that projected an image of its surroundings onto a surface through a small hole. It wasn't until the early 19th century that this concept transformed into something more tangible and purposeful with the invention of the pinhole camera. The pinhole camera functions on a straightforward principle: light enters through a tiny aperture into a dark chamber, creating an inverted image on the opposite side. This primitive tool laid the groundwork for capturing images, heralding the birth of what we now recognize as photography.

As a budding photographer myself, I find immense intrigue in this simplicity. I remember building my first pinhole camera during a high school science project. The materials were rudimentary—a cardboard box with a pinhole made from a needle and a piece of photographic paper inside. The anticipation of capturing an image with such simplicity was palpable. After a few hours of exposure to sunlight, we developed the paper in a dark room, revealing the first photograph I had ever taken. It was a blurred image of my backyard, yet to me, it was pure magic. That experience ignited my love for photography and set me on a path to explore its deeper nuances.

The next significant leap in the evolution of photography came with the introduction of glass plates, which provided a more stable medium for capturing images. The daguerreotype process, developed by Louis Daguerre in 1839, was the first commercially viable method of photography. It utilized a polished silver plate coated with light-sensitive chemicals, producing highly detailed images. This was a revelation at the time, as it allowed for the permanent capturing of moments that could previously only be rendered through art or memory. While these early photographs required long exposure times and elaborate setups, they established a profound connection between the photographer and their subject.

One of my favorite historical anecdotes relates to the portraiture of that era. Wealthy individuals commissioned daguerreotypes to immortalize their likenesses, while the less affluent sought out itinerant photographers who traveled from town to town. These photographers transformed people's lives through the lens by capturing the essence of who they were. Looking back, I see parallels in my own journey as I transitioned from shooting portraits of friends to documenting significant moments in community events. Each photograph tells a story, much like those early daguerreotypes.

As the 19th century progressed, advancements continued to shape the landscape of photography. The introduction of collodion in the 1850s marked another turning point. This wet plate process allowed photographers to produce clear, detailed images with shorter exposure times. The ability to capture moments spontaneously, rather than staging every shot, transformed photography. It inspired a sense of exploration and adventure among photographers as they sought to document life in its most organic forms. I often draw inspiration from this sentiment in my current work. Just as early photographers eagerly captured the world around them, I strive to observe and document the intricacies of everyday life through my lens.

The emergence of film in the late 19th century represented the next pivotal moment in photography. George Eastman's invention of roll film in the 1880s facilitated a shift away from cumbersome large-format cameras to more portable equipment. This innovation made photography accessible to the general public, birthing the phrase "You press the button, we do the rest." The Kodak camera popularized this accessibility, empowering amateur photographers to document their lives without needing technical expertise. The innate human desire to capture memories found its medium, creating a wave of interest in photography that was unprecedented.

Reflecting on my early experiences, I remember the excitement of using my first handheld camera—a point-and-shoot model gifted to me by my parents. It wasn't the most professional device, but it opened doors to my passion. The ability to take pictures of family gatherings, holidays, and nature during our summer vacations created a repository of personal history, allowing me to revisit moments that defined my life. This ability to effortlessly capture and share memories not only impacted my life but altered the very fabric of society and culture, where photos began to impact narratives and influence perspectives.

With the turn of the 20th century came further innovations, including color photography. While experiments with color had been taking place since the early days of photography, it wasn't until the development of Kodachrome film in the 1930s that color photography became widely available. This technological leap shifted the visual storytelling landscape dramatically, as photographers no longer relied solely on black-and-white images to evoke emotions and narrative depth. The vibrancy of color allowed for more expressive storytelling, capturing the nuances of life in ways that black and white could not.

During my early college days, I explored the world of color photography through various assignments and projects. I vividly remember the first time I developed my own color film. It felt like unveiling a treasure, where each print revealed bright hues and shades, breathing life into the scenes I had captured. This process—so tactile, so hands-on—established a deeper bond with the artistic endeavor of photography. Each image encapsulated the emotions of the moment, a instant connection of feelings enhanced by the use of dynamic colors.

The 1960s and 1970s brought a wave of motion within the photography world. Cameras became more versatile, and the introduction of the 35mm format enabled photographers to experiment with different lenses and techniques. Pentax, Canon, and Nikon emerged as trailblazers, creating equipment that met the needs of a growing community of enthusiasts and professionals alike. Alongside these advancements, the rise of documentary photography emphasized the role of the photographer as a storyteller, with iconic figures like Henri Cartier-Bresson and Dorothea Lange paving the way for visual journalism. As I immersed myself in these stories, I developed a profound respect for the power of the image to enact social change and foster awareness.

I often consider the ramifications of these pioneers in shaping my own narrative as a photographer. Their unwavering commitment to capturing the human experience resonates deeply with my own motivation. On several occasions, I have sought to mirror their ideals in my work—whether it be through street photography or documenting social issues in my community. Each encounter presents an opportunity to connect, to understand, and to share stories that might otherwise go unheard.

The transition from film to digital photography in the late 20th century marked one of the most transformative periods in the evolution of photography. The development of digital cameras, starting with the first model introduced by Nikon in 1988, revolutionized the field. Photographers now had the ability to capture high-quality images instantly and manipulate them with editing software. The shift to digital brought about an unprecedented level of accessibility, creativity, and experimentation. Images could be shared in real time across digital platforms, catalyzing the rise of photography as a favorite medium for self-expression.

I experienced this shift firsthand. My first digital camera, a modest compact model, opened up new possibilities for exploration. The absence of film constraints meant I could shoot freely, test techniques, and play with concepts without the fear of waste. I remember attending my first photography workshop where we were encouraged to embrace the digital age fully. Capturing a moment and viewing it within seconds was exhilarating. Sharing gardens, selfies, and landscapes with friends online became inherent parts of daily life, redefining how we interact and connect.

As digital photography became more sophisticated, the integration of technology accelerated. The introduction of smartphones equipped with high-quality cameras revolutionized how and where images were taken. Photography became more than a hobby; it turned into a collaborative social experience. People shared their lives through pictures on platforms like Instagram, reshaping culture in profound ways. The boundaries drew closer; no longer required to invest in expensive equipment, anyone could claim the title of photographer.

My engagement with digital photography reshaped my understanding of the art itself. I found myself increasingly immersed in the digital community and reflecting on the shift in perception of the medium. I often engaged in discussions about the implications of digital technology on authenticity and creativity. While the digital boom democratized photography, it also gave rise to new challenges—image saturation, manipulation, and evolving definitions of artistry. In the flux of these discussions, I sought balance by focusing on capturing genuine moments and honing my individual style.

Even as technologies evolved, the raw emotion embedded within a photograph remained timeless. Each new innovation sought to elevate and amplify the narrative, allowing photographers to connect with viewers on deeper levels. However, the essence of photography—the capability to convey stories, emotions, and messages—endured. This realization deepened my commitment to using the lens not just as a tool, but as a means of connecting with humanity and exploring shared experiences.

As we navigate through this fascinating journey from the pinhole camera to digital imagery, it is essential to recognize the impact of technological advancements on our understanding and engagement with photography. Each innovation reflects the desires and aspirations of the time, bringing forth new opportunities and challenges for photographers. This evolution is not merely a timeline of inventions; it embodies the shared human experience, encouraging reflection on our own journeys and memories captured through the lens.

Photography is arguably one of the most influential arts that bridges the gap between time and emotion. Each image we gather shapes our understanding of our surroundings and ourselves, documenting life in its myriad complexities. As you embark on your photographic journey or reflect on your experiences, consider how these technological shifts have influenced your perspective in the world of photography. Each period of evolution invites us to adapt and innovate, inspiring us while reminding us of our role as visual storytellers armed with the power of the lens.

The Impact of Technology

As the sun dipped below the horizon, casting a warm amber hue over the bustling streets, I stood with my camera in hand, contemplating the profound changes technology had brought to photography. It struck me how far we had come since the days of film and darkrooms; how the world of photography was no longer confined to the exclusivity of professionals but had become an accessible art form for anyone with the desire to see through a lens. Digital technology has been the catalyst for this transformation, enhancing creativity and allowing diverse voices to tell their stories.

In the early days of photography, capturing an image was a meticulous process that required skill, patience, and significant financial investment. Film was expensive, and each shot counted; minor mistakes could mean wasted resources. As I navigated through this landscape, I often heard seasoned photographers lamenting how digital cameras would ruin the craft. However, as I delved deeper into the realm of digital photography, I began to understand that the perceived drawbacks could also be viewed through the lens of opportunity.

One of the most significant advantages of digital technology is the democratization of photography. The barriers that once separated aspiring photographers from the world of imaging have largely dissipated. The advent of affordable digital cameras and smartphones equipped with high-quality cameras has empowered countless individuals to express themselves creatively. Today, anyone can capture moments, edit images, and share them instantly, all at their fingertips.

Renowned photographer Jasmine Star expressed this sentiment perfectly: "Photography is a universal language. With each image, we break down barriers and connect with others." This connection fosters a community of photographers from diverse backgrounds, sharing unique perspectives and experiences. The vibrant online photography communities bloomed, with social media platforms such as Instagram, Flickr, and 500px allowing users to showcase their work and engage with fellow photographers globally.

Moreover, the ease of sharing images online has transformed how we perceive photography. The once solitary endeavor now exists in a social context where photos can be evaluated, critiqued, and celebrated in real-time. This immediacy can act as a double-edged sword; while it allows photographers to gain exposure and feedback rapidly, it can also cultivate a culture of comparison and unrealistic standards. The constant barrage of perfectly curated feeds can lead to self-doubt and a sense of inadequacy to many budding photographers who may feel overwhelmed by the apparent perfection surrounding them.

Despite this, technology has significantly amplified creativity. Digital editing software, such as Adobe Photoshop and Lightroom, offers tools that were once reserved for a select group of professionals. Now, whether you are subtly enhancing colors, correcting flaws, or creatively altering images, the possibilities seem limitless. This access to sophisticated editing tools allows photographers to realize their vision without the constraints of traditional methods.

I remember a time when I struggled with a landscape photograph that felt lackluster. The scene was beautiful, bathed in an ethereal glow, but the image didn't translate the way I had envisioned. Rather than mourning my defeat, I turned to editing software and spent hours experimenting with contrast, saturation, and highlights. The moment I pulled the slider to enhance the vibrancy of the colors, my image transformed. It changed from a passive snapshot to a vivid representation of the emotions I felt during that moment. I realized that technology was not merely a tool but a medium that allowed my artistic vision to flourish.

However, as we embrace these digital advancements, we must also acknowledge their potential drawbacks. The convenience offered by technology can lead to complacency. With the ability to take hundreds of photos in a single shoot, it can be easy to lean on the buffer of digital storage rather than honing one's skills in composition, lighting, and timing. The challenge of digital photography is finding the balance between utilizing technology and preserving the artistry intrinsic to the craft.

Photographer David duChemin captured this tension succinctly when he said, "We are not a product of our technology, but we are shaped by how we choose to use it." His words serve as a powerful reminder that technology should enhance our creative process rather than dictate it. It's not merely about having the best gear or the latest software; it's about the story we tell through our images.

I recall attending a workshop led by an accomplished photographer who emphasized the importance of intentionality in our work. "Every shot should be crafted as if you were working with film," he said. "Take a moment to breathe, to observe, to think before pressing the shutter." His perspective prompted me to reevaluate my approach to digital photography. I began to set deliberate intentions for each shoot, considering the narrative I hoped to convey, rather than getting lost in the number of images I could capture.

As our relationship with technology evolves, it is essential to engage critically with it. Reflecting on how devices and software shape our creative choices can lead to a more conscious practice.

How are you utilizing technology in your photography? Are you leaning into the ease it provides, or are you using it to push boundaries and explore new avenues of creativity?

Additionally, the advancements in technology have led to the rise of AI (artificial intelligence) in the world of photography. Software that analyzes images and suggests enhancements can be a valuable ally, yet it also raises questions about creativity and ownership. Is an image as individual if it's been significantly altered or enhanced by algorithms? This debate presents a unique opportunity for introspection as photographers navigate the relationship between human intention and machine assistance.

Creativity, after all, is not solely about the technical aspects but about the intent behind the image. The heart of photography lies in the emotions it evokes and the stories it tells. As we engage with technology, let us remain rooted in our purpose as storytellers. As the great photographer Henri Cartier-Bresson once said, "Your first 10,000 photographs are your worst." His words urge us to embrace the journey of improvement, acknowledging that each image, regardless of its technological enhancement, adds to our personal growth.

It's crucial to remember that photography is an evolving art form. The impact of technology on photography is profound, shaping both accessibility and creativity in unprecedented ways. As we continue to navigate this evolving landscape, let us engage mindfully with technology, crafting our artistic vision through the lens of both technique and emotion.

In reflecting on my own photographic journey, I see how technology has influenced not only my work but also my relationship with fellow photographers. Digital platforms have allowed me to connect with others, sharing experiences and learning from diverse perspectives. I have engaged in spirited discussions with photographers from around the world—each sharing their triumphs, failures, and insights into the craft. These dialogues have deepened my understanding of photography and encouraged me to embrace experimentation in my work.

As I continue down this path, I ask myself: How do I wish to define my relationship with technology? Will I allow it to shape my creativity, or will I use it as a tool to enhance my voice? This question is one every photographer must confront, recognizing the delicate balance between embracing innovation and preserving the essence of what it means to create art.

The tools at our disposal today open up a world of infinite possibilities. Digital photography has empowered photographers to capture and share their visions in ways that were previously unimaginable. However, this new era also requires us to consider our motivations, our connection to our subjects, and how we engage with the stories we wish to tell. We must remain vigilant and intentional, ensuring that our technological advancements do not overshadow our artistry and voice.

The evolution of photography through technology has created an exciting landscape filled with opportunity and creativity. This new age encourages us to explore the world around us, to capture moments in time, and to share them with a global audience. As we embrace these changes, let us find joy in the act of creation and continue to push the boundaries of our art, ensuring that the essence of photography—the very heart of storytelling—remains intact.

The Future of Optical Technology

The realm of photography is in the midst of a seismic shift, driven by technological advancements that continuously redefine our understanding and utilization of optical technology. As we gaze into the future, it is essential to not only recognize the emerging trends in camera design, lens technology, and artificial intelligence but to also envision how these innovations will shape our creativity and practice as photographers.

At the forefront of these advancements is the evolution of camera design. We have long transitioned from cumbersome film cameras to sleek, digital models that boast incredible capabilities. However, the next generation of cameras is not merely a facsimile of its predecessors; it represents a profound reimagining of what a camera can be. With the integration of artificial intelligence, cameras are becoming increasingly intuitive, allowing photographers to focus on their artistic vision rather than wrestling with technical limitations. For instance, machines now possess the ability to discern subjects in a frame, adjust settings in real-time based on lighting conditions, and even offer composition suggestions. This transformative change allows both amateur and professional photographers to capture exceptional images with minimal effort.

One striking example of this trend is the emergence of computational photography, which utilizes algorithms to enhance photographic images significantly. Companies like Google and Apple have led the charge in integrating this technology into consumer devices such as smartphones. The iPhone's Night Mode, for instance, employs computational techniques to capture multiple frames in low-light situations and merge them into a singular, remarkably detailed image. This innovation has revolutionized night photography by eliminating the need for bulky equipment and extensive technical know-how. As computational photography continues to evolve, we can anticipate even more sophisticated algorithms that will further enhance image quality, allowing photographers to capture visually stunning photographs in previously unfeasible conditions.

Parallel to the evolution of camera design is the advancement in lens technology. As optical designs become more complex and refined, we are witnessing an incredible expansion in lens capabilities. The introduction of variable-aperture lenses, which seamlessly adjust their aperture based on light conditions, marks a significant leap forward. This flexibility not only enhances exposure but also allows for greater creative control over depth of field and motion blur. Manufacturers are increasingly focusing on developing lightweight, compact lenses that are capable of delivering exceptional image quality, making them ideal for on-the-go photographers who refuse to compromise on performance.

Moreover, innovations such as hybrid lenses, which combine traditional optical elements with digital enhancements, are gaining momentum. These hybrid lenses can reduce visual aberrations and improve overall image clarity, pushing the boundaries of what is achievable in photography. Photographers can now create images with unparalleled sharpness, color accuracy, and dynamic range, all while maintaining the compactness and adaptability that modern lifestyles demand.

Artificial intelligence is not just transforming cameras; it is also reshaping the very way we engage with our photographic practice. AI-powered editing tools are streamlining post-production workflows, making it faster and more intuitive to enhance images. Programs like Adobe Lightroom and Photoshop are increasingly incorporating AI features that allow photographers to automate tedious tasks such as retouching and color correction. These innovations provide artists the freedom to focus on their creative instincts rather than being bogged down by the meticulous details of the editing process.

Yet, as we embrace these advances, we must also consider the implications they carry. The democratization of photography has been accelerated by the rapid integration of these technologies, allowing a wider array of individuals to explore the craft. While this proliferation can enrich the art form with diverse perspectives, it simultaneously raises questions about authenticity and the essence of traditional photography. As our tools become more sophisticated in their ability to create and manipulate images, we may find ourselves navigating a landscape where the line between genuine artistry and artificial enhancement becomes increasingly blurred.

To inspire readers to think outside the box, it is vital to showcase innovative photographers in our rapidly evolving field. One compelling case study is that of the renowned photographer, Jerry Uelsmann, who has pushed the boundaries of photographic expression for decades through his surreal, multi-exposure images. Although Uelsmann mainly worked with traditional film, his philosophy about merging multiple visions can resonate with modern creators who use digital editing tools. He serves as a testament to the endless possibilities of visual narrative, encouraging photographers to explore the intersections between technology and artistry.

In contemporary times, the work of Jessica Eaton exemplifies the innovative spirit of photographers adapting to new technologies. Eaton's playful and meticulous exploration of color and light is achieved through the use of both analog and digital techniques. By harnessing her knowledge of optics and the capabilities of digital editing software, she has created mesmerizing visual experiences that challenge our perception of color and space. Her work invites photographers to redefine boundaries by interrogating the relationship between technology, reality, and their personal vision.

As we look further into the future, we will witness the advent of augmented reality (AR) and virtual reality (VR) in photography itself. These technologies have the potential to create immersive experiences, allowing viewers to engage with photographs in new and interactive ways. Imagine stepping into a photograph, experiencing it in a 360-degree environment, and even immersing yourself in the story behind that image. Photographers will have the opportunity to create narratives that unfold not just through a single frame but through layers of visual storytelling, inviting viewers to become participants in the experience.

Moreover, 3D printing technology may well become an avenue for photographers seeking to materialize their visions in novel forms. Artists could create sculptural representations of their images, forging deeper connections between the medium of photography and tactile, tangible art. By exploring uncharted territory in both form and presentation, photographers can continue to evolve their practice, challenging perceptions and reaching wider audiences.

As we move forward, it is imperative that photographers remain adaptable to the ever-changing landscape of technology. Engaging with emerging tools, experimenting with new genres, and forging meaningful connections with their subjects will ensure that creativity and authenticity continue to thrive amidst the digital tide. These challenges also serve as opportunities for growth as we seek to evolve with, rather than resist, the changes taking place within photography.

In conclusion, the future of optical technology promises a wealth of innovation that will reshape our understanding and engagement with photography. By embracing advancements in camera design, lens technology, and artificial intelligence, photographers have an unprecedented opportunity to redefine their creative practices. We invite you, the reader, to immerse yourself in this rapidly evolving field and explore how these emerging trends can enhance your artistic vision. Let the stories of innovative photographers inspire you to think beyond the limits of your current practice and envision a future that harmonizes technology and artistry. The landscape may be shifting, but the heart of photography remains steadfast—our desire to connect, communicate, and capture the essence of life through our lenses.

CHAPTER 3

COMPOSITION: THE ART OF ARRANGEMENT

Principles of Composition

The art of composition in photography is akin to the blueprint of a building; it lays the groundwork for a photograph, guiding the viewer's eye and helping to convey the story behind the image. As photographers, understanding the principles of composition is essential in creating compelling visuals that resonate with viewers on both emotional and aesthetic levels. In this subchapter, we will delve into the fundamental principles of composition: the rule of thirds, leading lines, and framing techniques. Through visual examples, personal anecdotes, and practical exercises, you will gain a deeper understanding of how to apply these principles in your own photographic practice.

The rule of thirds is arguably the most well-known principle of composition. It serves as a foundational guideline that helps photographers create balanced and engaging images. To apply the rule of thirds, imagine dividing your frame into nine equal parts using two horizontal lines and two vertical lines. The points where these lines intersect are called "power points." Placing key elements of your photograph along these lines or at these intersections can create a sense of harmony and focus, allowing the viewer's eye to move naturally throughout the image.

During my early days as a budding photographer, I vividly recall my first encounter with the rule of thirds. I was attending a local photography workshop, eager to absorb every bit of knowledge I could. The instructor handed each participant a checklist, emphasizing the importance of composition. On that list, the rule of thirds was at the very top. With my camera in hand, I wandered through a nearby park, looking for subjects to capture. I scrutinized every scene, attempting to consciously place my subjects in line with the rule of thirds.

One of my favorite photographs from that day features a solitary tree standing in a vast field of green grass. I positioned the tree along the left vertical line, while the horizon stretched across the middle horizontal line. The result was an image that felt dynamic yet harmonious, providing ample negative space for the eye to breathe. The rule of thirds transformed what could have been a standard snapshot into a thoughtfully composed photograph that drew viewers in.

While the rule of thirds is a powerful tool, it is essential to remember that it is just that—a tool. Sometimes rules are meant to be broken. As you grow in your craft, you may find that other compositions better express the stories you wish to tell. Next, let's explore the concept of leading lines. Leading lines are an effective way to guide the viewer's eye through your photograph, creating a pathway that draws attention to the main subject. These lines can be found in various forms—roads, rivers, fences, or even the contours of a person's body. The key is to leverage their natural directionality to create depth and interest.

I had a particular experience that highlighted the power of leading lines while exploring an abandoned industrial site. The remnants of a rusted train track snaked through the grounds, weaving its way toward a distant horizon. I instinctively raised my camera, framing the track in the foreground and allowing it to lead the viewer's eye toward the back of the image. The juxtaposition of the weathered lines against the overgrown foliage created a story of decay and resilience. The leading lines not only guided the eye but also added a sense of depth and dimension to the photograph.

When applying leading lines in your own work, consider the following tips: First, look for natural lines within your environment. What elements can you incorporate into your frame that will lead the viewer's attention? Second, experiment with different angles and perspectives to enhance the lines within your composition. Sometimes, a simple shift in position can transform a flat photo into something vibrant and engaging.

Framing is another invaluable compositional principle that helps to draw attention to your subject. By using elements within your scene to create a "frame" around your subject, you can lead the viewer's eye toward the focal point of your image. Framing techniques can include natural elements such as branches, archways, or patterns found in architecture. By using these frames, you create a visual context that enhances the subject and provides a sense of depth.

A memorable moment I experienced while using framing occurred during a sunset shoot at a beach. I discovered a stunning natural arch along the coastline, carved by years of ocean waves. Instead of photographing the arch head-on, I crouched low and aligned it so that it framed a silhouetted couple walking hand-in-hand in the background. The natural arch not only added interest but also conveyed the intimacy of that moment, encapsulating a romantic connection between two people amidst nature's beauty.

Framing can also elevate the storytelling aspect of your photographs. When considering framing techniques, ask yourself: What elements in your environment can serve as a visual frame for your subject? How can the frame enhance the mood or narrative of your image? The answers to these questions may lead you to surprising and compelling compositions.

To further illustrate the application of these principles, let's dive into a series of practical exercises designed to reinforce your understanding and help you analyze your own images. These exercises invite you to observe your surroundings through a new lens, encouraging you to consider how composition plays a role in your photographs.

First, take a stroll in a local park or your neighborhood. Observe your environment and identify elements that can serve as leading lines or frames. Spend at least an hour capturing various subjects, consciously applying the rule of thirds, leading lines, and framing techniques. After your shoot, review the images you captured and select three that resonate the most. For each photograph, write a short paragraph reflecting on how you utilized the principles of composition. Consider what worked well, what could be improved, and how the composition tells a story.

Another exercise involves exploring different compositions in one location. Choose a spot that offers diverse subjects—perhaps a market, a busy street corner, or a natural landscape. Spend time photographing the same scene from multiple angles and viewpoints. Challenge yourself to create images that incorporate the rule of thirds, central composition, and various framing techniques. Once you have a collection of images, analyze each photograph by noting how composition impacted the final result. This exercise not only enhances your technical skills but also hones your ability to see potential in ordinary scenes.

A third exercise encourages collaboration with fellow photographers. Team up with a friend and embark on a photo walk where each person takes turns choosing locations and subjects. Encourage each other to discuss composition principles during the shoot, offering feedback on how to enhance each other's images. By sharing ideas and perspectives, you can gain insights into how composition varies based on individual styles.

As you explore these exercises and reflect on your findings, remember that the principles of composition are not rigid rules but rather guidelines that can elevate your photography. Allow yourself to experiment with these concepts and discover how they can enrich your storytelling.

Embracing the principles of composition will significantly influence the way you perceive and create photographs. As you integrate these techniques into your practice, you will develop a keen sense of awareness that leads to more intentional compositions. This newfound focus will empower you to express your artistic vision more effectively, drawing viewers into the worlds you create through your lens.

In conclusion, the principles of composition, including the rule of thirds, leading lines, and framing techniques, serve as vital tools for photographers. By understanding and applying these concepts, you can craft images that are not only visually appealing but also rich in narrative and emotion. Through personal anecdotes and practical exercises, I hope to inspire you to embrace these principles in your own photographic journey. Remember, the art of composition is a continuous learning process. Let your experiences shape your perspective, and allow your creativity to flourish as you capture the beauty that surrounds you.

Advanced Composition Techniques

Composition is often regarded as the backbone of photography, the framework upon which beautiful images are built. As photographers progress beyond the basic principles of composition, it is vital to explore more advanced techniques that can elevate their work to new heights. In this subchapter, we will delve into concepts such as symmetry, balance, and the use of negative space. These techniques can transform ordinary images into compelling visual narratives that resonate with viewers on a deeper level. By embracing both victories and mistakes along the journey, photographers can refine their skills and develop a unique artistic style.

To begin, let's explore symmetry and how it can create a sense of harmony and order in an image. Symmetry can be classified into two categories: reflective symmetry and rotational symmetry. Reflective symmetry occurs when one side of the composition mirrors the other, whereas rotational symmetry involves repetitive elements that rotate around a central point.

Reflective symmetry is often found in landscapes, architecture, and nature. For instance, when photographing a calm lake at sunrise, capturing the reflection of the trees and mountains on the water's surface can create a stunning symmetrical composition. This principle not only enhances aesthetic appeal but also draws the viewer's eye to the symmetry, invoking a sense of calm and balance.

In my earlier endeavors as a photographer, I often overlooked the power of symmetry. During a trip to a stunning botanical garden, I spotted a beautiful flower arrangement. In my eagerness to capture it, I framed the shot slightly off-center, neglecting its inherent symmetry. The resulting image lacked the depth and visual harmony I desired. It wasn't until I re-evaluated my perspective and returned to the same spot that I realized my mistake. This time, I positioned myself directly in the center of the flower bed, allowing the symmetry of the blossoms to shine through. The final image exuded elegance and tranquility, reinforcing the idea that composition mistakes can lead to powerful learning moments.

As we hone our skills in symmetry, we should also embrace the concept of balance. Balance involves distributing visual weight throughout a composition, creating a sense of equilibrium. Too often, photographers place their subject matter in a predictable position without considering how the elements surrounding it influence the overall image. There are three primary types of balance: symmetrical balance, asymmetrical balance, and radial balance.

Symmetrical balance reflects the earlier discussion on symmetry, wherein both sides of the composition mirror each other. However, asymmetrical balance provides a different dynamic. This type of balance occurs when different elements of varying visual weights create equilibrium in a non-mirrored arrangement. For example, consider an image of a lone tree standing against a vast horizon. While the tree represents a heavy visual anchor on one side, the opposite side might consist of a sprawling sky filled with soft clouds, distributing the visual weight evenly.

During an outdoor event, I captured a moment of a couple dancing in a lively celebration. Initially, I framed the image with the couple in the center, flanked by colorful balloons on either side. However, I noticed the composition felt heavy on one side, with all the attention drawn to the couple without enough balance. I repositioned myself to place the balloons on the left and the couple on the right, but the balloons were smaller in scale. This asymmetrical arrangement created more balance and added interest, as the background balancers engaged viewers while allowing the couple to remain the focal point. This experience taught me that balance doesn't always mean equal size; rather, it's about the effective distribution of visual elements.

Radial balance, on the other hand, involves elements radiating from a central point. This technique is particularly effective in capturing subjects such as flowers or circular architecture. As I explored botanical gardens, I often experimented with radial balance. One day, I came across a stunning flower in full bloom, surrounded by petals that created an almost circular formation. By capturing this arrangement with myself positioned directly above the flower, I was able to enhance the radial balance. The result was a captivating image that drew the viewer's eye inward, creating an aura of tranquility.

Another powerful advanced composition technique is the use of negative space. Negative space refers to the area surrounding the subject in a composition. Contrary to the traditional notion that only the subject matters, negative space can breathe life into an image by providing context and allowing the subject to stand out more distinctly.

Consider a simple photograph of a person standing on a vast beach. The person is positioned toward one side of the frame, while the expansive stretch of sand and ocean fills the remaining space. This negative space allows the viewer's gaze to appreciate the subject while contemplating the vastness of their surroundings. When I captured a moment of my friend walking along the shoreline, I chose to include a significant portion of the open beach in the frame. The resulting image conveyed a sense of solitude and freedom, emphasizing both my friend and the overwhelming beauty of nature.

To practice this technique, I encourage readers to identify potential subjects with ample negative space in their environment. Experiment with framing your subject with various backgrounds and settings, allowing negative space to unfold in unique ways. By consciously incorporating negative space, you will develop a more refined approach to composition, allowing the elements of your images to coexist harmoniously.

When exploring advanced composition techniques, it's essential to foster a sense of experimentation and creativity. Mistakes are inevitable along the way, but recognizing them as opportunities for growth can lead to incredible advancements in your work. Strive to challenge yourself during your photography journey, pushing the boundaries of your comfort zone.

In the spirit of experimentation, I propose several practical challenges to help you grasp these advanced composition techniques more profoundly:

1. **Symmetry Challenge:** Find a location that offers potential opportunities to capture symmetry. This might be a park, a street, or a piece of architecture. Experiment with different angles. Take multiple shots of symmetrical subjects, analyzing which angles create a stronger sense of harmony. Reflect on your favorite image and consider how symmetry adds value to your work.

2. **Balance Challenge:** Seek out a scenario that allows you to incorporate both symmetrical and asymmetrical balance. For instance, photograph a scene with a prominent subject on one side and additional elements on the opposite side to create balance. Afterward, compare your images—note which compositions feel balanced and which do not. What adjustments can you make to improve those unbalanced shots?

3. **Negative Space Challenge:** Go for a walk in your local environment, aiming to find subjects with ample negative space. Capture various compositions, experimenting with the proportion of negative space relative to the subject. Later, analyze the images—consider how different levels of negative space affect overall impact and emotion. What did you learn from this exercise?

4. **Radial Balance Challenge:** Seek opportunities in nature or architecture that allow you to experiment with radial balance. Photograph subjects that exhibit a circular or radial structure,

such as flowers or circular buildings. Consider the effect of different vantage points on the radial balance in your work. Did you discover new perspectives you hadn't considered before?

5. **Shooting the Ordinary:** Take a day to explore your environment and photograph mundane subjects. Look for angles that create symmetry, balance, or negative space from subjects that might ordinarily be overlooked. This exercise will compel you to see beauty in simplicity through the lens.

As you embark on these challenges, remember that the journey often entails trial and error. Embrace missteps and learn from them; they can lead you toward unexpected revelations about your artistic approach.

In my own journey, I found numerous moments of inspiration amid missteps. I once attempted to photograph an iconic landmark during a festival, teeming with colorful stalls and people. I hurriedly captured various shots, but many images lacked focus and failed to convey the vibrancy of the scene. However, in reviewing my shots, I spotted an image I had captured as an afterthought—a simple perspective of a vendor serving snacks against a blurred backdrop of festival-goers. This image stood out due to its framing and the way the vendor emerged from the chaos. The composition was instinctual; I was simply inspired by the moment, inadvertently employing the technique of leading lines created by the festival stalls behind him.

From that day forward, I made a conscious effort to assess my compositions critically, seeking greater balance and emotional connection. My earlier mistakes became valuable lessons that fueled my growth as a photographer.

As this subchapter closes, I invite you to reflect on your composition adventures. The exploration of advanced techniques, such as symmetry, balance, and negative space, is ongoing. Each photograph is an opportunity to tell a story, an invitation to experiment, and a chance to capture the essence of a moment.

Remember that progress comes not only from achieving perfect images but also from learning through practice, experimentation, and ultimately, embracing the beautiful imperfections of your personal photographic journey. Allow yourself the freedom to explore these advanced composition techniques without the pressure of perfection, and you may find that the most significant lessons arise when you most fervently consider the craft of photography and its myriad compositional possibilities.

Creating Impactful Images

The significance of composition in photography transcends mere aesthetics; it plays a vital role in conveying emotions and evoking responses from viewers. As photographers, we possess the power to guide the viewer's eye and shape their experience through deliberate compositional choices. In this subchapter, we will explore how the arrangement of elements within a frame can evoke a multitude of feelings, from serenity and joy to tension and unease. Through personal anecdotes, we will illustrate the direct correlation between composition, mood, and storytelling, empowering you to harness this knowledge in your work.

Composition is not simply about following rules; it is about making conscious decisions that reflect your artistic vision. As you engage with the world through your lens, consider the emotions you wish to evoke and how your compositional choices can support that intent. A photograph is a narrative in a single frame, and the way you compose that narrative can significantly alter its impact.

Reflecting on my early experiences as a photographer, I recall one instance that taught me the profound emotional weight of composition. During a long-awaited trip to the coast, I set out to capture the sunset over the ocean. As the sun began its descent, the sky exploded into vivid hues of orange, pink, and purple. Eager to document the beauty, I set up my tripod, envisioning the idyllic shot with the setting sun directly in the center of the frame, surrounded by the waves crashing on the shore.

However, as I began to press the shutter button, doubts crept in. I recalled my mentor's advice: "Don't just position your subject in the center. Think about the story you want to tell." I stepped back, adjusting my angle and incorporating more of the foreground into the composition. With the sun anchored off-center, the crashing waves created a leading line that drew the viewer's gaze towards the horizon. The resulting image expressed a sense of tranquility, yet it also captured the fleeting beauty of the moment—reflecting both the serenity of the ocean and the urgency of time passing.

This experience highlights how changing the composition not only alters the visual but deeply affects the emotion that the photograph embodies. Centered compositions can often feel static, limiting the narrative potential. In contrast, off-center compositions can introduce dynamism and encourage viewers to explore the image. Thus, it becomes essential to recognize how various arrangements not only relate to aesthetic principles but also serve as conduits for emotional expression.

Different compositional strategies can yield varying emotional effects. The Rule of Thirds is a foundational principle that suggests dividing your frame into a grid of nine equal sections, positioning points of interest along the lines or at their intersections. This method often creates a balanced yet dynamic composition, guiding the viewer's eye naturally.

For example, positioning a subject on one of the grid's intersections can create a sense of imbalance, leading to feelings of tension or anticipation. In my portrait works, I often employ this technique to portray subjects in a more contemplative or introspective state. When I included a subject looking away from the camera, gazing into the distance on a lower third line, the resulting image conveyed a rich narrative of longing, stirring viewers to engage with the subject's emotional context.

On the other hand, symmetrical compositions evoke a sense of order and calmness. By centering your subject symmetrically, you can create a harmonious and stable image. During a recent project in a quiet woodland, I encountered a stunning symmetrically placed tree with its reflection perfectly mirrored in a still pond. By capturing this scene with a symmetrical composition, I conveyed a sense of tranquility and balance that mirrored the serenity of the setting.

However, it is crucial to note that emotional responses can be subjective. Additionally, the viewer's background, values, and experiences influence their interpretation of your images. Thus, it becomes essential to approach your compositions from an emotional standpoint while remaining cognizant of the myriad perspectives of your audience.

Exploring negative space is another powerful compositional technique to evoke emotion. Negative space refers to the area surrounding your subject, often acting as a contrast that amplifies the subject's presence. When photographing landscapes or portraits, incorporating negative space can evoke feelings of isolation, solitude, or freedom.

Last summer, in an expansive desert landscape, I captured an image of a solitary figure standing against the vastness of the dunes. By leaving ample negative space surrounding the subject, I emphasized their insignificance against the enormity of the landscape, which instilled a sense of wanderlust and introspection. The emotional impact of the photograph was amplified by this careful arrangement— encapsulating the extraordinary within the ordinary.

In contrast, filling your composition with subjects and details can generate intensity and energy. When documenting a bustling market scene, allowing chaos into your frame can evoke feelings of excitement and vibrancy. During my travels, I ventured into a vibrant open-air market filled with colors, sounds, and people. By capturing a close-up image of local spices in overwhelming detail, I transformed an ordinary commodity into a textured experience, conveying the richness of culture and community.

Among the lesser-explored aspects of composition is the influence of leading lines. Leading lines serve as visual pathways that direct the viewer's gaze throughout the image. Roads, rivers, and architectural elements can create a sense of depth, drawing viewers into the photograph. When hiking in the mountains, I encountered a winding path that lead through a dense forest. Framing the path as a leading line in my composition instilled a feeling of adventure and exploration, inviting viewers to journey alongside.

As you engage with composition, reflect on your experiences and consider how you can use these principles to translate your artistic vision into impactful images. It isn't only about recognizing these techniques; it's about understanding how they resonate with you emotionally and how you can impart that emotion onto your audience.

Practical exercises can further enhance your ability to make conscious compositional choices. One exercise to consider is setting a specific emotional intention before you capture an image. Take a moment to think about the feeling you want to evoke—be it joy, solitude, or excitement. As you shoot, consciously apply compositional strategies aligned with that emotional goal.

For instance, if your intention is to evoke joy, seek out bright colors and playful interactions. Use dynamic angles and off-center compositions to create an engaging visual narrative. Alternatively, if you seek to capture solitude, explore negative space and subdued color palettes, focusing on simplicity and minimalism. Reflect on the resulting images and how they align with your emotional intentions.

Another exercise involves creating a diptych or triptych that showcases different compositional choices to convey varying emotions about the same subject. Select a singular theme—such as a person, place, or event—and photograph it in different ways. Create a heavily structured, symmetrical composition alongside a dynamic, off-center arrangement. Analyze how each composition influences the narrative and emotional undercurrents of the series.

Additionally, consider joining community critiques where you share your work and receive feedback. Engaging with fellow photographers can provide fresh perspectives on your compositional choices, enabling you to refine your vision while considering the emotional impact of your images.

Ultimately, the intersection of composition and emotion is a rich field for exploration. By being deliberate in your arrangements, you hold the key to infusing your photographs with storytelling potential. Each composition is a choice that comes from a place of intention, allowing you to evoke empathy, inspire reflection, or ignite curiosity in your viewers.

As you evolve as a photographer, allow your vision to grow through observation and experimentation. Embrace the challenges that come with exploration, whether through compositional missteps or the serendipity of unexpected arrangements. Every frame is an opportunity not only to capture a moment but also to invite viewers into a shared emotional experience.

In conclusion, it is essential to blend technical knowledge with personal insights as you construct your visual narratives. The emotional impact of your compositions will ultimately shape how your work resonates, inviting viewers into a conversation with each image. Embrace composition as a vital storytelling tool that can bring depth, nuance, and emotion into the world you capture through your lens. As you continue your journey in photography, remember that every composition is a unique reflection of your artistic vision—make it a memorable one.

CHAPTER 4

LIGHT: THE PHOTOGRAPHER'S PAINTBRUSH

Understanding Natural Light

As I stood beneath an autumn canopy, the late afternoon sun filtered through the trees, casting a warm golden hue that transformed the landscape into a luminous painting. This moment was not merely a series of random occurrences; it was a perfect melding of light, nature, and my camera, each element playing a distinct role in the creation of an evocative photograph. Natural light is perhaps the most potent tool in a photographer's arsenal, shaping not only the aesthetic quality of an image but also the emotional narrative it conveys.

Understanding natural light begins with an appreciation of its fleeting nature. Unlike artificial light, which can be controlled and manipulated, natural light is unpredictable; it ebbs and flows, dictated by the time of day, weather conditions, and location. Early morning light, often referred to as the "golden hour," casts long shadows and bathes the world in soft, diffused tones. Conversely, the starkness of midday sun—while bright and vibrant—can create harsh shadows and unflattering contrasts, making it challenging to capture a subject's true essence.

In the beginning of my photographic journey, I often found myself drawn outside at dawn, captivated by the soft pinks and oranges that heralded the day. I remember one particular morning at the beach, where the rise of the sun mirrored the awakening of life around me. Silhouettes of surfers preparing for the first waves contrasted with the luminous reflections dancing on the water's surface. It was a moment of serene beauty, where every element—the surf, the sky, the sun— seemed to sing in harmony. The natural light allowed me to capture the stillness of the moment while simultaneously injecting energy and anticipation into the image.

Over the years, I have encountered a myriad of lighting conditions that have tested my understanding and adaptability. On one occasion, I trekked into the mountains for a landscape shoot, armed with my camera and an ambitious vision in mind. As I reached the summit, a dense fog rolled in, consuming the world around me. Initially frustrated, I soon realized that this weather was an opportunity rather than a setback. The diffused light created an ethereal atmosphere, transforming the stark cliffs into ghostly figures, their details softened and muted. By embracing the fog and its accompanying light, I was able to produce a series of photographs that conveyed a sense of mystery and introspection, something I might never have achieved under clearer skies.

These experiences have taught me the importance of assessing lighting conditions and adapting my approach accordingly. A key aspect of mastering natural light is learning to visualize how different elements interact. For instance, the position of the sun—whether rising, setting, or at its zenith—dramatically alters the quality of light. The "golden hour," occurring just after sunrise and before sunset, should be a staple in every photographer's schedule. During this time, light is much more forgiving, casting soft shadows that enhance form and texture while enveloping subjects in a warm glow. In contrast, shooting around noon, when the sun is high, presents unique challenges. This harsh overhead light may require adjustments in posture and angle, as well as a keen eye for finding shade or incorporating reflective surfaces.

Clouds can also be best friends or worst enemies, adding another layer of complexity to natural light. A cloudy day creates a softbox effect, diffusing light and minimizing shadows, which can be ideal for portrait photography. I often found myself gravitating toward locations with overcast skies, as this type of light enables me to illuminate the contours of a subject's face while eliminating the harsh contrasts found on sunny days. Take, for example, a portrait I shot during a spring day with a group of children playing in a park. The subtle natural light created a gentle and tranquil scene, allowing the children's laughter and expressions to shine through without the distraction of strong shadows.

Moreover, reflecting surfaces can dramatically affect the way we perceive light. Water, glass, and even sand can reflect, diffuse, and shape light in unexpected ways. On one occasion, while photographing a lake at sunset, I discovered how the shimmering water served as a mirror, capturing the vibrant colors of the sky and amplifying the beauty of the scene. Instead of merely framing a sunset, I was able to produce an image that became a dialogue between the heavens and the earth, where one influenced the other.

Understanding light involves not just observation but also execution. Here are specific tips to help assess and utilize natural light effectively for storytelling in your photography:

1. Observe the Shadows: Shadows can add depth and dimension to an image. Assess the direction, length, and intensity of shadows to guide your compositions. Use shadows creatively to enhance textures, portray drama, or establish a mood.

2. Watch the Weather: Each weather condition creates unique lighting opportunities. Fog can create a dreamlike effect, rain can enhance color saturation, and snow can reflect light beautifully. Make note of how the atmosphere affects your subject matter.

3. Experiment with Direction: The angle from which light hits your subject can influence how it is perceived. Side lighting can emphasize textures and create drama, while backlighting can produce a halo effect that adds ethereal quality to an image. Constantly test different angles until the light aligns with your vision.

4. Use Reflectors: Natural reflectors, like sandy beaches or open fields, can help bounce light back on your subject. Learning to

utilize reflectors effectively opens up new possibilities and can dramatically improve your images.

5. Be Mindful of Time: Time of day considerably impacts light's character. Plan your shoots around sunrise and sunset for optimal lighting conditions, but remain flexible to capture unusual lighting moments occurring at any time.

6. Patience is Key: Sometimes, waiting for the right lighting conditions can yield the most stunning images. As a general rule, if the light isn't right, be patient and watch how it changes before making a decision.

The emotional resonance created by natural light involves much more than mere observation. It's about allowing the light to influence your vision and intentionality in the moment. During one particularly transformative experience, I journeyed to a local coffee shop one rainy afternoon, my camera slung over my shoulder and my objective unclear. As I entered, I was struck by how the ambient light filtered through the windows, muted yet inviting. I decided to capture the essence of the place—the coziness, the warmth, the shared stories. Without a clear plan, I wandered, taking shots of patrons lost in moments of solitude, laughter, and conversation.

The images reflected the emotions enhanced by that particular light: the soft rain against the glass creating a blurred separation between inside and out, inviting viewers to step into an intimate narrative. Each frame intertwined the relationships of light, space, and subject, creating a tapestry of human experience.

Every photographer has a unique relationship with light, shaped by individual style and perspective. As you embark on your own photographic journey, I encourage you to reflect on how light has influenced your work. Consider keeping a journal to document your thoughts and feelings about light in your images, exploring how certain lighting conditions have shaped your storytelling.

As you experiment with light, cultivate a sense of playfulness and curiosity. Challenge yourself to capture the same scene at different times of the day, or during varying weather conditions. Each iteration presents an opportunity for discovering new narrative layers, revealing the transformative power of light that can turn a simple scene into a compelling story.

In conclusion, the beauty of natural light lies in its ability to transform our perception and experience of the world. By understanding its nuances and embracing the spontaneity it brings, we open ourselves to more profound artistic expression, allowing our imagery to leave a lasting impact on viewers. Whether capturing the gentle glow of dawn or the dynamic dance of shadows at dusk, remember that light is not just an element in photography—it is the very essence that breathes life into our art. Embrace it, experiment with it, and let it guide your lens as you forge your path in the inspiring realm of photography.

Artificial Light Techniques

As photographers, we often find ourselves at the mercy of natural light. The soft glow of the golden hour, the harsh glare of the midday sun, or the moody ambiance of twilight each provide unique opportunities to capture stunning images. However, understanding and mastering artificial light opens a whole new realm of creativity and expression. This section serves as your gateway into the world of artificial lighting techniques, where the control is in your hands, and the creative possibilities are limitless.

Artificial lighting can come in many forms, but the two most popular types are flash (or strobe) and continuous lighting. Each has its advantages and disadvantages, and understanding these can help you select the best tool for a given situation.

Flash photography is characterized by a brief pulse of light, usually emitted in one burst; it's versatile and can be used in various settings, from portraits to event photography. A speedlight, which is a small, battery-powered flash unit, is commonly attached to the camera or used off-camera to create dramatic light effects. The sudden burst of light can freeze motion, enabling you to capture fast-moving subjects with clarity. However, mastering a speedlight requires practice; the nuances of sync speed, power settings, and modifiers add layers of complexity that can intimidate novice photographers.

I still remember my first experience with flash photography. Eager to capture my friend's wedding, I confidently set up my portable speedlight, excited for the possibilities. However, the wedding venue was dimly lit, and after several frames, I realized my settings were all wrong. My subjects appeared like ghostly silhouettes against an overly bright backdrop. After some humbling trial and error, I learned that adding diffusion materials softened the harshness of the flash, resulting in a more natural look. This lesson changed the way I approached flash photography. I began to view it not as a tool to battle darkness but as a means to sculpt light.

Continuous lighting, on the other hand, provides a constant source of illumination, allowing the photographer to see exactly how the light interacts with the subject in real time. This can simplify the shooting process significantly, especially for beginners still grappling with the intricacies of flash sync. Continuous lights can come in the form of LED panels, tungsten lights, or fluorescent fixtures, each offering unique color temperatures and intensities. While these lights allow for easy adjustments and real-time previews, they can generate heat, require careful handling, and are less portable compared to flash units.

The first time I experimented with continuous lighting was during a studio shoot for a local band. I had set up softbox lights to create a warm, inviting atmosphere, but as we progressed, I realized that the mix of lights I was using didn't match in color temperature. The result was a jarring combination of yellow and blue casts across the images. Faced with this challenge, I quickly learned about the importance of color balance, so I spent time researching gels and filters to create uniform light sources. It was a worthwhile journey, as my output not only improved, but I began to appreciate the creative potential of color contrast and harmony in my work.

Now that we've established the basic types of artificial lighting, let's delve into techniques for effectively harnessing their power.

One essential technique is lighting direction. The angle of light plays a critical role in shaping the look of your photograph. Front lighting creates a flat aesthetic, often popular for product photography, whereas side lighting adds dimension and depth, revealing textures in your subject. Backlighting can create silhouettes or highlight translucent objects effectively, crafting that magical rim light that gives images a professional touch.

Consider a portrait session. If you were to use front lighting with a flash positioned directly in front of your subject, you might capture even illumination on their face, producing a straightforward shot. But if you shift the flash to a 45-degree angle, the light casts shadows across their features, enhancing their cheekbones and creating a more three-dimensional feel. Experimenting with the positioning of your artificial lights can breathe life into your images.

Another powerful tool in your lighting arsenal is diffusion. Softening the source of your light can create a more natural feel. While strobe lights produce a harsh beam, incorporating diffusion materials like softboxes, umbrellas, or even a sheet of white fabric can transform your flash into a beautiful, gentle light source. I remember an outdoor portrait session in harsh sunlight where I set up a softbox to diffuse the midday rays. The resulting portraits were ethereal, the light wrapping around my subject delicately and creating pleasing skin tones. The produced glow felt friendly and inviting, prompting viewers to connect with the image on a deeper level.

In contrast, if your creative vision requires stark, high-contrast images, consider using bare flashes for dramatic shadows. This technique is especially effective for editorial or fashion shoots. One of my favorite experiments involved processing a model for a fashion series, using hard light pant roof-mounted speedlights positioned to one side. The resulting images had a raw, emotive quality that resonated with the theme of rebellion I was aiming to pursue.

Color gels are another avenue for creativity. They add vibrancy and drama to your images. By placing colored gels over your flash or continuous lights, you can introduce hues that enhance the mood of your photographs. You could experiment with a blue gel to produce a tranquil feel or a red gel for an electrifying vibe. During a promotional shoot for a local theater, I incorporated these gels to match an autumn-themed production. The results were spectacular, adding depth to the ambiance that would have otherwise been lost with standard lighting.

For our next practical exercise, you'll be diving into the world of color gels. Choose a subject to photograph, it could be a friend, a beloved pet, or even an everyday object around your home. Set up both flash and continuous lighting. Begin with natural light, capturing an initial image to establish your baseline. Then, select two or three color gels to experiment with.

Start with one color gel at a time, adjusting your lighting source's distance from the subject to see how this affects color saturation and shadow placement. Feel free to use multiple gels, layering them over each light if your equipment allows. After your experiment, review the images—note how the different colors influence mood, mood, and visual story, and determine which combinations resonate with you.

Light modifiers don't end with diffusion and gels; they include reflectors as well. A reflector bounces light back onto your subject, filling in shadows and adding highlights, effectively broadening your control over the illumination in your scene. During a product shoot, I experimented with a gold reflector for a series of accessories. While the flash created hard shadows, the reflector helped soften their intensity, giving the items a luminous quality.

To better understand the relationship between light and shadow, another exercise can be beneficial. Set up a simple still-life scene using artificial light. Place your subject so that the primary light source is at a 45-degree angle, creating defined shadows. Move the reflector around: place it close, then far away, and observe how the shadows respond. Capture a series of images that document the variations, helping you afford deeper insights into how subtle adjustments affect illumination dynamics.

Post-processing plays a crucial role in leading your viewer's gaze, adjusting tone, and enhancing emotion. Artificially lit images can lend themselves to compelling edits, particularly in terms of color correction. With your raw files, experiment with adjusting the color balance and tweaking shadows and highlights to emphasize your intended look.

As you conquer different techniques, you'll find your unique style emerging. My personal journey with artificial light has been one of self-discovery, pushing artistic boundaries and reshaping my perspective of what light can accomplish.

Capture daily life and the moments that matter most. Set aside time to shoot under artificial light, away from natural conditions. Explore unconventional indoor locations and experiment boldly. Follow contemporary photographers who specialize in artificial lighting, absorbing their stylistic choices.

Cultivating this ability grows not merely from understanding equipment; it stems from fearless exploration and experimentation. As your experience deepens, you'll refine your voice and find confidence in your artistic vision. Consider how you would engage with a subject, lighting a story uniquely tailored to them. Your images will tell their tale via the language of light.

Once you feel comfortable with artificial lighting techniques, your photography will transcend the ordinary and invite viewers into a vivid world of light and emotion. Throughout the journey, recognize that every setback is an opportunity for growth, every misfire teaches invaluable lessons. With each session, your ability to capture the essence of a moment will solidify as you learn to paint with light, framing your artistic endeavors in a new, vibrant spectrum.

As you move forward, keep pushing the boundaries. Try new equipment, explore different genres of photography, and collaborate with fellow photographers. Take them along on your lighting ventures, discuss techniques, and challenge each other as you work on projects that inspire creativity. Each shared experience will only refine your understanding and enhance your artistic vision.

Artificial lighting is your paintbrush—wield it with intention, and every photograph will become a masterpiece that speaks to the power of light and storytelling in ways you've yet to explore. Embrace the challenge, find joy in the process, and let your creativity shine.

The Emotional Impact of Light

In the world of photography, light is more than a simple necessity for exposure; it is an artist's brush, shaping the form, texture, and warmth of an image. Just as a painter mixes different paints to evoke emotions on canvas, photographers manipulate light to render feelings through their work. Each encounter with light offers a new opportunity to tell a story, to evoke a sense of place, or to capture a fleeting emotion.

As a young photographer, I often found myself enchanted by the golden hues of the evening sun. The way it warmed the skin of my subjects or danced across the landscape felt almost magical. I remember a particular moment that solidified my appreciation for the emotional power of light. It was an autumn day, the air crisp with the promise of winter. I had ventured out to a local park, my camera slung around my neck, searching for scenes that encapsulated the essence of the season. As I rounded a bend, I stumbled upon a little girl playing with her dog. Gentle rays of sunlight streamed through the branches of a nearby oak tree, setting the scene aglow with warmth.

The girl laughed as her dog chased the falling leaves, her joy contagious. In that moment, bathed in golden light, everything aligned perfectly. I pressed the shutter, freezing the laughter, the warmth, and the vivid colors of autumn in a single frame. When I look back at that photograph, I don't just see the image; I feel the warmth of the sun on my skin and hear the laughter echoing in my mind. That photograph serves as a reminder that light can evoke memories and emotions just as profoundly as the subject itself.

Understanding how different sources and qualities of light can impact the mood of an image is essential for any photographer. Natural light, whether it is the soft pastel hues of dawn or the harsh glare of midday sun, creates distinct atmospheres. For instance, soft, diffused light, such as that found on an overcast day or during the golden hour, casts a gentle glow that can evoke serenity or nostalgia. Conversely, hard, direct light can evoke tension or drama, sharpening the contrasts and creating striking shadows.

In the realm of portraiture, the emotional resonance of light is even more pronounced. I recall a portrait session with a friend who was experiencing a challenging period in her life. I found a spot in her garden where the late afternoon sunlight filtered through the leaves, creating a delicate pattern of light and shadow on her face. As I adjusted my camera, I noticed how the soft light suited her emotional state, transforming the image into an intimate portrayal of vulnerability. The shadows under her eyes captured the weight she was carrying, while the light illuminating her smile reflected the glimmers of hope she still held onto. The photograph told a story that was not just visual but deeply personal, rooted in the emotional nuances of that moment.

These experiences remind us that beyond technical proficiency, photographers have a responsibility to discern the emotional qualities of light. When I teach workshops, I often encourage my students to pay attention to how they feel as they observe light in their surroundings. Is the light harsh or soft? Is it warm or cool? How does it interact with the subject? By inviting this level of awareness, we open ourselves to creating narratives that resonate beyond the surface of our images.

Moreover, the interplay between light and shadow can profoundly affect the emotional weight of a photograph. Shadows are not merely the absence of light; they can add depth and intrigue. Consider the dramatic portraits of classic Hollywood photography. The use of shadow to contour the face enhances the sense of mystery and allure, creating iconic images that linger in our minds. I remember an evening spent experimenting with low-key lighting in my studio. I directed a single light source at my subject, allowing deep shadows to carve out her features. The resulting images were hauntingly beautiful. The shadows whispered stories of resilience and strength, while the light illuminated hope and vulnerability. Here, light and shadow had crafted a compelling narrative that went beyond the physical appearance of the subject.

As photographers, we wield light with intention, channeling our creative vision into each frame. It is essential, then, to consider how we can manipulate light to strengthen our storytelling abilities. One practical exercise involves choosing a subject and deliberately using various light sources to capture different emotional tones. For instance, photographing a landscape at sunrise might highlight tranquility and renewal, while the same scene at dusk could evoke introspection and melancholy. By observing the emotional shifts prompted by each lighting condition, you will cultivate a profound understanding of light's role in visual storytelling.

To further explore this concept, I suggest a hands-on exercise involving shadow play. Choose a subject—this could be a person, an object, or a scene—and set up lighting in such a way that shadows become a key feature of the image. Play with the direction of light, adjusting its intensity and source. Notice how shadows alter the perception of your subject. For instance, if you illuminate your subject from below, it can create an eerie or surreal atmosphere, contrasting against the more familiar overhead lighting. This exercise encourages you to embrace experimentation, allowing you to discover how shadows enhance the story you wish to convey.

Another captivating exploration involves capturing light and its emotional essence at different times of day. Morning and evening offer unique qualities that can transform an ordinary scene into something extraordinary. A photograph taken during the golden hour—just after sunrise or before sunset—can imbue an image with warmth and nostalgia. The air is softer, almost ethereal. On the contrary, high noon delivers bright, unforgiving light, which can bring a sharpness and vibrancy that, when embraced, can convey a sense of urgency or intensity.

Consider a personal project that documents the same scene at various times of day. This could be a favorite park, a bustling street corner, or your own backyard. Capture the same composition in the morning, noon, and evening, observing how the changing light influences the mood. Reflect on your emotional response to each photograph and what each time of day reveals about the subject. This exercise will not only enhance your technical skills but deepen your appreciation for the emotional tapestry that light weaves through your images.

As we explore the emotional impact of light, it's also crucial to understand the psychological effects of color temperature. The warm tones of sunset evoke feelings of comfort and nostalgia, while cool tones, like those found in the shadows of a winter day, can inspire feelings of calmness or even sadness. Recently, while photographing a winter scene blanketed in snow, I was struck by the contrast between the soft blue light of the overcast sky and the warm glow of a distant sunset. The combination of these colors created a striking emotional narrative—the cold, harsh reality of winter contrasted with the fleeting warmth of a setting sun.

As you venture into your own photography, consider how you can utilize color temperature to evoke specific emotions. Set aside time to explore different light sources and their temperatures—incandescent bulbs, daylight, tungsten light. Pay attention to how they influence the perception of your subject. Document your findings and reflect on how color temperatures align with the feelings you wish to convey.

In addition to color and intensity, the mood created by the quality of light forms an inseparable part of emotional storytelling. Soft light, produced by diffusers or cloudy conditions, may evoke feelings of tenderness and calm. In contrast, harsh light can instigate unease or tension. I often experiment by photographing the same subject in varied lighting conditions to uncover narratives I might not have envisioned initially. One time, while shooting a still life, I used a simple table lamp to create a defined beam illuminating objects on my table. The hard shadows and stark contrast provided a sense of drama, transforming mundane objects into a captivating tableau. The play of light breathing life into what seemed like a static arrangement was a exhilarating reminder of the transformative power of light.

The intentional creation of light can also guide us toward deeper emotional connections with our subjects. The experience of helping someone feel comfortable in front of the camera is influenced heavily by lighting. When working with portrait subjects who may feel apprehensive, I often employ soft, flattering light, such as that from a large softbox, which diminishes shadows and produces a gentle glow. This nurturing quality of light fosters a relaxed atmosphere, encouraging authenticity. As thoughts return to the portrait session I had with my friend, I cannot help but remember how her expressions shifted in response to the light surrounding us. When she felt the warm sun kissing her cheeks, her laughter was brighter, her smile more genuine. The light created a connection that transcended the lens, revealing her spirit in its most radiant form.

Light has a power that can instigate not only emotion in an observer but also a connection between the photographer and subject. Thus, exploring different lighting setups can be an invaluable exercise in fostering empathy and understanding. A project that involves shooting a series of portraits focusing solely on the emotional qualities of light can be illuminating—literally. Experiment with different light sources, reflecting how each lighting condition affects your subject's expression and mood.

Furthermore, reflect on your own emotional responses to the captured images. What feelings emerge when you view these portraits? Are certain subjects more expressive under specific lighting conditions? Participation in these kinds of exercises not only hones your photographic skills but cultivates an emotional resonance between you and the images you create.

Finally, as we conclude this exploration of the emotional impact of light, I encourage you to embrace a mindset of exploration and experimentation. Photograph in different settings, manipulate your light sources, and observe the narratives that unfold before you. As you interact with light, notice how it shapes not just the aesthetics of your photographs but the very emotions they evoke.

Create a small portfolio featuring images that resonate with specific emotions tied to light—be it joy, nostalgia, vulnerability, or strength. Acknowledge the role that light plays in each story you wish to convey. This portfolio can serve as a poignant reminder of light's power, both in your own journey as a photographer and in the hearts of those who view your work.

Light is not only a tool; it is a storyteller, an emotion, and an experience. It guides observers through the stories captured in our frames, enabling them to feel rather than just see. As you journey through your photographic practice, may you continue to embrace this power and harness the emotional resonance of light in your work, creating images that speak volumes long after the shutter clicks.

CHAPTER 5

EMOTION IN EVERY FRAME

The Essence of Emotion

As a photographer, I often find myself pondering the essence of emotion in every frame I capture. It's a concept that transcends mere technical skill, diving deep into the realm of human experience. This subchapter aims to explore the techniques for authentically capturing emotion in photography, drawing upon personal anecdotes and insights that speak to the often-elusive nature of feelings in imagery.

Emotion is the heartbeat of photography. It transforms a straightforward documentation of events into a resonant story, capable of striking a chord with viewers. My journey in understanding this began during my early days as a budding photographer when I realized that capturing genuine feelings requires more than just pressing the shutter at the right moment. It demands an intricate dance between empathy, patience, and keen observation.

One vivid memory stands out—a candid shot that I captured at a bustling street festival. The sun had begun to set, casting a golden glow over the crowd, but it was a single mother sitting on a bench displaying her emotions that drew me in. She was watching her child play, a mix of pride and joy on her face, yet there was a fleeting shadow of worry in her eyes. As I approached her, I felt an instinctive pull to document that moment.

I held back, observing her without intruding, keenly aware that the authentic emotion I sought might vanish if I stepped too close too soon. I watched as she smiled brightly at her child but also fought back tears, perhaps reminding herself of struggles that lay just beneath the surface. With my camera ready, I took a deep breath, calmed my own racing heart, and clicked the shutter just as a child's laughter exploded beside her. The frame encapsulated pure, unfiltered emotion—a testament to the magic of observation and the importance of patience.

This particular experience led me to understand that emotion in photography is not always about setting up the perfect shot; it's often about allowing moments to unfold naturally. The pressure to elicit emotion can paradoxically create distance between the photographer and the subject. This became evident in my portrait sessions, where I would strive to create compelling, emotional images. I found that the authenticity of emotion often requires a level of trust between the photographer and the subject.

A notable example involved a portrait session with an elderly man named Mr. Thompson, whose face bore the intricacies of a lifetime. As I set up my equipment, I could sense his discomfort. Despite my efforts to engage him in light conversation, he remained tense, visibly hesitant to open up. It was then that I decided to try a different approach. I ditched the formalities, asking him instead about the love of his life, a woman he had lost many years prior to illness.

To my surprise, his demeanor shifted dramatically. Memories danced in his eyes as he recounted stories that took him back to a time filled with joy and heartbreak. Suddenly, he was no longer Mr. Thompson, the subject of my portrait; he was simply a man revisiting cherished memories. As I captured his candid expressions— moments of laughter, nostalgia, and heartfelt sorrow—I felt the atmosphere around us transform. It was in that shared space of vulnerability that we created an image that portrayed his essence, rich with emotion and story.

Through these experiences, I've come to appreciate that emotion, much like light in a photograph, can be subtle or glaring, yet it always brings depth to an image. The act of capturing emotion does not solely rely on momentary pressings of the shutter, but rather on the dialogue, the back-and-forth, the connection formed in that fleeting moment.

Additionally, the way we present our subjects can amplify or diminish the emotions we aim to convey. When photographing a moment of joy, it might be beneficial to allow figures in the frame to spread apart, hands extended or laughter radiating outward. Conversely, a moment of solitude or reflection can be heightened by bringing the subject closer to the edges, isolating them against a blurred backdrop. Each choice in composition directly influences the emotional interpretation of a photograph.

The most profound lessons in capturing emotion often come not from failed attempts, but from adventures that did not go as planned. In one session, I prepared to capture a couple celebrating their anniversary. Expecting a playful, romantic atmosphere, I had envisioned soft light, laughter, and prominent closeness between the subjects. However, as we began, the mood shifted unexpectedly. The couple had recently had a tumultuous argument that hung thick in the air.

Initially, I thought the mood might ruin the shoot as they stood stiffly, struggling to smile for the camera. But rather than pressing for forced affection, I engaged them in an open dialogue. We spoke about the beauty in imperfections, and suddenly the tension began to lift. Laughter, genuine and raw, pierced through the remnants of earlier discord, leading to a series of beautifully candid moments. By embracing the discomfort and allowing their emotions to flow freely, I was able to capture a depth of feeling that I wouldn't have achieved had I insisted on a "perfect" facade.

With every frame, patience was my greatest ally. The fleeting nature of emotions makes it crucial to remain observant and ready to seize the moment. It is all too easy for feelings to evaporate in a heartbeat, leaving behind only a husk of what once was. Therefore, I encourage readers to take your time—watch and wait for just the right moment. Focus intently on how it feels to be in the space you occupy with your subject. Emotions can be incredibly nuanced, and they often blossom in the most unexpected moments.

Reflective prompts can serve as valuable tools to cultivate this awareness in photography. Consider the following:

1. What emotions do you wish to evoke through your imagery? Is it joy, sadness, nostalgia, or perhaps resilience? Think about specific moments that evoke these feelings within you and why they resonate.

2. When shooting candidly, how can you become a better observer? What techniques can you use to blend into the background, allowing your subject's feelings to emerge without pressure?

3. In portrait photography, how can you facilitate a more trusting atmosphere with your subject? Reflect on the importance of dialogue and connection when capturing emotion.

4. Reflect on a moment when a photo you captured didn't meet your expectations at the time. How did the circumstances surrounding that image shape its emotional context?

As we develop our understanding of capturing emotion in photography, it is crucial to remember that every photographer's journey is unique. Your emotional landscape may differ significantly from someone else's, and that diversity of perspective brings richness to photography. Each heartfelt encounter or moment of vulnerability you document adds to the tapestry of human experience, allowing others to feel connected through your images.

In the end, capturing emotion in photography is about more than just the photograph itself; it's about the human experience shared in that moment. The authentic stories you tell will resonate much longer than the pixels captured in your frame. So, as you continue your journey, nourish the patience, practice observation, and open your heart to the myriad emotions that define our lives. The essence of emotion will weave its way into your photographs—and into the hearts of those who view them—creating an unbroken link between the viewer, the subject, and the world you are capturing.

Telling Stories with Emotion

The essence of photography lies not only in capturing moments but also in evoking emotions—transforming mere images into powerful stories that resonate with viewers. Each frame has the potential to transport the observer into the depths of human experience. Emotional imagery transcends language barriers, stirring feelings that connect people through shared experiences. In this subchapter, we will explore the narrative aspect of emotion in photography, delving into iconic photographs that have left an indelible mark on our collective consciousness. We will also reflect on the process of crafting emotionally charged images, highlighting personal stories that illustrate the journey of translating raw feelings into visual art. By the end, you will be equipped with exercises designed to refine your ability to tell stories through the lens, guiding you to create a series of images that explore a specific emotional theme.

Photography has an uncanny ability to capture the ephemeral nature of emotion. Whether it's a joyous celebration, the weight of sorrow, or the quiet grace of solitude, an impactful photograph can encapsulate profound feelings in an instant. One iconic example is the photograph "Afghan Girl" by Steve McCurry, which graced the cover of National Geographic in 1985. The piercing green eyes of Sharbat Gula, a young Afghan refugee, reveal a deep well of emotion—fear, resilience, and uncertainty. McCurry's careful attention to her gaze, coupled with the desaturated colors of her surroundings, conveys both the fragility of her situation and the strength within her. This image has become a symbol of the refugee experience, emphasizing how a single photograph can tell an expansive story that resonates for decades.

Emotionally charged images hold the ability to spark dialogue and inspire action. For example, consider Kevin Carter's haunting photograph from the 1993 Sudan famine, which depicts a starving young girl being watched by a vulture. The power of this image lies not only in its shocking content but also in the overwhelming sense of helplessness and urgency it conveys. Viewers are confronted with the stark reality of suffering and the moral dilemmas that arise from such disparities. Carter's photograph transcends mere documentation; it serves as a catalyst for discussions around humanitarian aid and global responsibility, making viewers aware of the broader narrative surrounding such crises.

The act of telling stories through imagery requires the photographer to engage empathy and vulnerability in their work. Personal experiences often translate into deeper connections with subjects, allowing photographers to capture emotions that resonate on a universal level. One of my own pivotal moments occurred during a photo session with a group of elderly women from my community. I had been commissioned to capture portraits for a local charity project aimed at celebrating their lives and experiences. As I listened to their stories, I found myself drawn into their lives—each woman had a unique journey shaped by triumphs and hardships, laughter and sorrow.

During the session, I aimed not merely to capture their physical likeness but to encapsulate their essence. After some initial poses, I encouraged them to share more of their stories, revealing layers of laughter, tears, and memories. One woman, in particular, spoke of losing her husband and the profound loneliness that followed. As I listened to her voice crack with emotion, I instinctively adjusted my camera settings to encapsulate the moment—not just her physical features but the sheer weight of her narrative. The resulting portrait encapsulated her vulnerability, evoking compassion from anyone who laid eyes upon it. This experience solidified my belief that a photograph can tell a story far beyond what is seen; it can communicate the soul of a person experiencing life in all its complexity.

As storytellers behind the camera, we must often step beyond our comfort zones and embrace the emotional nuances of our subjects. This act of vulnerability opens pathways to authenticity in our work. Consider the emotional landscape depicted in the photographs of renowned photojournalist Dorothea Lange. Her image "Migrant Mother," taken during the Great Depression, captures a moment of profound despair and resilience. The expression of a mother, surrounded by her children, reflects a mix of worry, strength, and determination. Lange's ability to capture this depth of emotion speaks not only to her skills as a photographer but also to her commitment to understanding her subjects.

Reflecting on our own storytelling journeys begins with considering the emotions we wish to evoke. Understanding the themes that resonate with us as individuals can direct our photographic practice and allow us to explore emotional narratives. When I first embarked on focusing my work on themes of isolation and connection, I found inspiration in everyday moments and interactions. A simple gesture—a hand reaching out to another—became a powerful visual motif that conveyed warmth and vulnerability. Documenting such moments sparked conversations about human connectivity, allowing viewers to reflect on their own experiences related to isolation.

It's vital to ask ourselves: What stories do we want to tell through our photography? When crafting emotionally evocative series, consider starting with a specific theme. For example, if you find yourself drawn to themes of joy, explore events like weddings or family gatherings, capturing candid interactions that radiate happiness. Hone in on details—awkward laughter, shared glances, and moments of spontaneity. Conversely, if you gravitate towards themes of sorrow, aim for spaces that evoke these feelings. Perhaps a local park with benches that convey solitude or an empty street after rain can serve as a background for capturing reflective moments that resonate with melancholy.

To develop a series that encapsulates your theme, consider these exercises designed to evoke emotion and narrative depth in your work:

1. **Emotion Mapping**: Begin by selecting an emotion that resonates with you—joy, sadness, nostalgia, or anger. Write down a list of visual metaphors or objects associated with that emotion. For instance, if you choose nostalgia, consider images of old family photographs, faded letters, or abandoned places. Create a shot list or storyboard outlining potential images that convey this emotion visually. Spend a week seeking out and

capturing these elements, allowing yourself to iterate and refine your artistic vision.

2. **Candid Capture Challenge**: Engage in a candid photography challenge where you photograph the day-to-day lives of those around you—friends, family, or even strangers. Set aside a two-hour window and immerse yourself in their world, capturing moments that convey genuine feelings. Reflect on how spontaneous interactions can tell stories, often revealing more than staged portraits.

3. **Thematic Self-Portrait Series**: Consider exploring your own emotions through self-portraits. Create a series that depicts various facets of your emotional journey—perhaps using props, lighting, and compositions that represent your inner state. For example, if you're exploring feelings of isolation, experiment with framing yourself in constrained spaces, using shadows to convey depth and mood. This exercise allows you to intimately examine and express your emotions while deepening your storytelling skills.

4. **Visual Storytelling Workshop**: Collaborate with fellow photographers or artists to host a workshop focused on visual storytelling through emotion. Share your thematic ideas and images, and invite feedback from peers. This collaborative environment can foster creativity and provide fresh perspectives on conveying emotional narratives.

The process of capturing emotion in photography is dynamic and ever-evolving. As photographers, we have the responsibility to approach our subjects with genuine curiosity and care. Behind every image lies a story waiting to be revealed, and it's our privilege to delve into the lives and emotions of those we photograph. Strong emotional imagery not only enriches our portfolios but also creates a lasting impact that transcends time and space.

As you embark on your journey of telling stories with emotion, remember that every frame is an opportunity to evoke feelings, provoke thought, and ignite conversations. The art of photography is rooted in our ability to foster connections—to ourselves, our subjects, and our viewers. Seek out stories that resonate with you; approach each encounter with an open heart and mind. Allow the emotional weight of your imagery to carry through, inviting viewers into the narrative tapestry that unfolds within each frame.

In conclusion, photography is not merely an act of capturing the fleeting moment but a profound exploration of emotion and storytelling. Iconic photographs resonate through time because they capture universal experiences—moments of vulnerability, resilience, and love. As you refine your practice, embrace the intricacies of human emotion, allowing it to guide your storytelling journey. By engaging deeply with your subjects and embracing authenticity in your style, your photographs will inevitably tell stories that resonate on a soul level, evoking the beauty and complexity of the human experience in every frame you capture.

Candid vs. Posed

Photography is a powerful medium for storytelling, and at its core, it often revolves around the portrayal of human emotion. One of the fundamental distinctions within this realm is the difference between candid and posed photography. Both approaches have their own unique merits and challenges, yet they share a common goal: to evoke emotion and convey a narrative through a still frame. In this exploration, I will delve into my personal experiences with both styles, illustrating how they can be utilized to capture raw emotion while also addressing the tension that often exists between spontaneity and control in photography.

Candid photography thrives on spontaneity. It invites moments that unfold naturally, capturing the essence of an experience as it happens. In those fleeting seconds when individuals are lost in thought, laughter, or a mere glance, the camera becomes a witness to authenticity. For me, some of my most treasured photographs stem from candid moments—those unexpected pixels of life that reveal deep emotional truths without contrivance. I remember a vibrant street festival I attended in the heart of the city. The sun was setting, casting a golden hue over everything it touched. As I wandered through the crowd, my lens caught sight of an elderly couple dancing together, their faces lit with joy. The tenderness they exhibited—their hands clasped, bodies swaying gently to the rhythm of a distant band—was astonishingly beautiful. I wasn't poised to capture their moment; rather, it unfolded before me organically, and I was simply there to capture it.

This spontaneity isn't always easy to achieve. It requires a degree of detachment from the final product, a willingness to let go of the rigid framework of composition, and instead, observe the world with a sense of curiosity. As a photographer, I often find myself becoming a silent observer, tracking the ebb and flow of human interaction. I strive to blend into the background, making my presence as inconspicuous as possible. However, there are challenges that accompany this style. One of the most significant hurdles is the unpredictability inherent in candid photography. Timing may elude you when shooting in dynamic environments, and missed moments can lead to frustration. Yet, there's sheer joy in that unpredictability, too; the thrill of never quite knowing what might happen next keeps the creative pulse alive.

Conversely, posed photography embodies intent. Each subject, each detail, is orchestrated with purpose. The photographer collaborates with their subjects, guiding them through the process to achieve a desired vision. Occasionally, a posed setting can lead to the creation of stunning images, capturing elegance and beauty that might not arise in the chaos of spontaneity. I recall a portrait session I did for a friend who was expecting her first child. She wanted something serene, artistic—far removed from the spontaneous chaos of everyday life. We spent a significant amount of time arranging the light, selecting outfits, and finding the right backdrop to convey the mood she desired. By carefully staging the scene and employing direction, we were able to evoke a sense of delicate anticipation in the finished images that truly reflected her emotions.

A challenge for posed photography often lies in authenticity. Subjects who may feel self-conscious or unsure of how to present themselves can appear stiff or unnatural. During our session, I noticed my friend becoming more comfortable, yet there were fleeting moments where the vulnerability of her anticipation was overshadowed by those carefully crafted poses. To counteract these instances, I've found it vital to create an environment that cultivates trust and ease, allowing subjects to shed their self-consciousness. Offering gentle promptings, encouraging laughter, or simply engaging in a conversation can often bridge the gap between being posed and feeling genuine. It's a delicate dance: one that must reconcile the photographer's intent with the subject's essence.

Both candid and posed photography have their homes in emotional expression, yet they achieve it in distinct ways. One is rooted in the beauty of unguarded moments, while the other thrives on deliberate storytelling. More often than not, my preference leans toward candid photography when seeking to capture emotion because of the authenticity embedded within those moments. However, I also recognize the pivotal role posed photography plays in intentional storytelling.

I remember attending an art exhibition that showcased a powerful series of posed portraits, where each subject directed their gaze towards the camera, but with varying expressions. The series tackled themes of identity and belonging, and the photographer manipulated each person's body language and setting to communicate different emotional narratives. The deliberate nature of these portraits elicited thoughtful engagement from the audience. I realized that even though the images were meticulously staged, they still resonated with the viewers on an emotional level. The tension between the controlled environment of posed photography encouraged a dialogue that mere candid shots sometimes lack.

Finding balance between these two approaches can further enrich one's photographic skills. An experiment I often recommend to photographers is to mix both styles within a single session. For instance, during a family gathering or an event, start with posed portraits that establish a sense of control, guiding subjects into thoughtful poses. Following these staged moments, transition into candid shooting—the balmy warmth of laughter, the children playing, glances exchanged in comfortable conversation. This juxtaposition allows for a comprehensive narrative that offers insights into the relationships and emotions within those gathered. When I applied this approach during a recent wedding shoot, I was able to showcase the joy of the couple through the grandeur of posed portraits while simultaneously capturing the raw emotions of laughter, tears, and exhilaration present throughout the day.

Encouraging readers to explore their preferences between these styles can be a path towards cultivating a unique voice within their photography. Every photographer occupies a space along the candid-posed spectrum. A challenge to undertake is to consciously choose a theme and approach it first through candid photography, then again through posed portraits. This will create an opportunity for self-reflection, allowing one to evaluate how different techniques can influence the story being told.

Candid moments and posed images each have their respective strengths, but their powers can be enhanced when used in tandem. Life isn't always predictable, and capturing it hinges on our emotional connections with our subjects. Sometimes, the most powerful shots emerge when subjects are unaware, lost in the moment. Other times, a carefully thought-out pose reveals a depth of feeling that transcends the visual capturing. The intersection of both styles emphasizes the diverse approaches possible within the realm of photography.

Moreover, the emotional weight an image carries is often informed by the concepts of trust and vulnerability. If a subject feels safe and comfortable, they are more likely to reveal their authentic selves—whether in a candid moment or during a posed engagement. Building that trust can be the linchpin to capturing deep emotion effectively. As photographers, it is our responsibility to create environments where individuals can let their guards down. When I reflect on my favorite shots, the threads that weave them together are formed by the connections established with my subjects. I strive to enter shoots with an attitude of mindfulness and empathy, acknowledging that I'm stepping into a moment that is meaningful to them.

As we navigate through our photographic journeys, a sense of curiosity coupled with an openness to experiment can reveal significant growth. The beauty of photography lies in its fluidity; it is not a rigid art form. Rather, it is a living exchange shaped by our interactions, emotions, and experiences. Whether I select to pick up the camera for candid shots or staged portraits, I remain committed to capturing the essence of humanity—the laughter, the tears, the connections that define us as individuals.

Both candid and posed photography invite exploration of emotion. In the tension between spontaneity and control, we as photographers discover greater depth within our work. There's beauty to be found in the flow of the unexpected as well as in the artistry of a well-crafted composition. This subchapter illuminates not only their distinctions but how they can harmonize intricately to shape compelling narratives. For readers, the true challenge will lie in their exploration of both, allowing each style to inform the other, ultimately leading to the emergence of a distinctive voice within their photographic artistry.

CHAPTER 6

THE DIGITAL REVOLUTION

The Rise of Digital Photography

The surge of digital photography has not only transformed the way we capture images but also redefined our relationship with the medium itself. As I reminisce about my early days behind a film camera, nostalgia washes over me—filled with the scent of developer fluid, the hum of the darkroom fan, and the careful anticipation that came with shooting a roll of film. The switch from film to digital wasn't just a technical upgrade; it was a profound shift in perspective, convenience, and creativity.

When I first picked up a camera, it was a Pentax K1000, a sturdy mechanical beast that welcomed the meticulousness of film photography. I enjoyed the tactile sensation of winding the film, hearing the click of the shutter, and the thrill of developing my own photos. Every frame felt precious—I was limited by the number of exposures per roll, encouraging me to consume each click intentionally. I learned how to look for light, understand composition, and observe the world around me. Each shot required a blend of patience and precision, as I sent my rolls to a lab, eagerly waiting days for the developed prints. In this environment, the art of photography felt sacred, preserved in time.

However, everything changed when I first held a digital camera in my hands—a Canon EOS 300D, a groundbreaking model that heralded the dawn of digital photography for enthusiasts like myself. At that moment, seamless instant gratification settled into my creative process. I could review each shot immediately, delete the mistakes, and reshoot without the looming pressure of wasting film. The first time I clicked the shutter and saw my image appear on the LCD screen felt like discovering a new world, unbound by the constraints I had previously navigated.

My transition from film to digital photography was met with an array of emotions. Initially, skepticism loomed over me. Could digital photography provide the same level of quality as film? Would my images still possess the rich tonal range, the organic grain, and the warmth that I so cherished? These questions peppered my early experiences, creating a hesitancy that needed to be addressed as I navigated the technical nuances of digital shooting. Learning about pixelation, sensor sizes, and the various file formats seemed overwhelming, and I often found myself yearn for the simplicity of film. Yet, as I practiced and grew, I began to appreciate the flexibility digital offered me—the ability to experiment with settings, shoot in RAW, and easily manipulate images in post-production.

Although my initial experiences with digital photography were challenging, I also celebrated numerous triumphs. The sheer volume of photographs I could take propelled my creativity to new heights. Where once I would think long and hard about each frame, digital encouraged a free flow of ideas and spontaneity. I stretched my legs and ventured into portraiture, street photography, and landscapes with fervor. Every outing with my digital camera felt like an invitation.

On an unforgettable summer evening, I strolled through a bustling farmer's market with a group of friends. The sun painted everything in brilliant golden hues, laughter echoed through the stalls, and the scents of fresh produce wafted through the air. I had my camera slung over my shoulder, automatically zoomed in and out of focus, adjusting settings on the fly. Capturing that moment was exhilarating; I could shoot as many frames as I wanted without anxiety, finally allowing myself to embrace the artistic chaos of the environment.

The transition to digital instilled in me a sense of immediacy that transformed my photographic eye. I became attuned to fleeting moments—expressions softened or erupted in laughter or a child twirling in jubilance while holding a bright balloon. The freedom to keep shooting without the worry of running out of film inspired a zest for life that was previously unexpressed. With each rapid click of the shutter, I unveiled a world filled with infinite possibilities.

As I navigated through my digital photography journey, I became more aware of the broader shifts occurring within the photographic community and culture. Digital photography not only created new opportunities for artistic expression but also democratized the medium, lowering the barriers to entry. More people could pick up a camera and share their perspectives, overthrowing the idea that photography was a realm reserved for professionals.

The dawn of social media accelerated this change, creating a vibrant space for photographers to share their work with diverse audiences. Platforms like Flickr, Instagram, and eventually TikTok gave rise to a new generation of visual storytellers. Social media transformed photography from a solitary practice into an interconnected dialogue between creator and viewer. It fostered a communal appreciation for the arts, where likes and comments could validate artistic endeavors and inspire collaborations across global communities.

As I experimented with my photography, I began to share my work online, and I quickly realized I wasn't just documenting my world but participating in the larger visual conversation. By sharing my photographs, I invited others to reflect on their experiences, sparking insight and relatability. I hark back to a comment I once received on an image of a weathered little girl holding a wilted flower. She said, "This reminds me of my childhood." In these moments of connection, I understood the power of storytelling through images.

I also observed the cultural shifts brought about by the proliferation of digital technology. The innovative capabilities of digital cameras made photography accessible to the masses. Suddenly, cameras were embedded in smartphones, turning everyday moments into spontaneous snapshots. People documented brunch gatherings, hiking adventures, and spontaneous outings, creating a digital scrapbook of their lives. This new form of connection changed how we interacted with memories—no longer confined to glossy prints in albums tucked away on bookshelves, these memories became instantaneously sharable.

However, while the rise of digital photography enabled broader participation, it raised conversations about quality versus quantity and the ethics of image manipulation. As the ease of taking and sharing images grew, so did concerns about authenticity and representation. The debate surrounding filters, photo editing apps, and the pressures of curating a perfect online persona became part of the fabric of contemporary photography culture. I found myself grappling with how best to strike a balance between enhancing images and remaining genuine in my storytelling process.

As I navigated this landscape, I embraced the concept of editing as an extension of my artistic vision rather than a means of masking imperfections. Post-production became an integral part of my photography workflow, where I experimented with contrasting colors, enhancing shadows, and exploring moods. Through editing, I learned to establish my style, consolidating my vision in a world saturated with images.

Ultimately, the conversation around digital photography encapsulates a larger societal narrative—a fusion of technology, creativity, and connection. Each image I captured was a representation of the present moment, rendered through my lens, yet embedded with the thoughts and emotions of a community that grew through shared experiences. My journey echoed the explorations of countless others navigating this digital realm.

Today, as I hold my digital camera and prepare to step back into the world, I recognize the value of reflection in enhancing my photography practice. I encourage you—my readers—to embrace your own journeys. Consider the moments and memories you were able to capture along the way, thanks to the rise of digital possibilities. Have you ventured into new creative territories as technology has evolved? How has your relationship with photography transformed with the advent of digital technology? Your experiences deserve exploration and expression.

As you explore the ever-expanding digital landscape, remember that every click of the shutter is a moment—one that speaks to your unique perspective and story. Celebrate the triumphs of engaging in this medium, the challenges that tested your resolve, and the collective cultural shifts that continue to shape the future of photography. Art is no longer just about capturing moments; it's about understanding the myriad of connections we forge through every image we create and share. In the end, digital photography invites us all to engage, connect, and embrace the beauty that lies in our stories.

Editing and Post-Production

In the realm of photography, the image you capture can often be seen as the beginning of a larger creative process. While the moment of capture is undoubtedly crucial, it is in the editing and post-production stages that your vision truly comes to life. As technology has evolved, so too have the tools at our disposal, enabling photographers to enhance their work in ways that were previously unimaginable. This subchapter will explore the world of editing, diving into various software, techniques, and personal anecdotes that illuminate the transformative power of post-production.

At the heart of editing lies the desire to refine and enhance. Whether it's correcting exposure, balancing colors, or cropping for better composition, editing serves as the bridge between the raw image and the final artwork. Every photographer has experienced the moment of staring at a photograph that feels almost, but not quite, what they envisioned. It is during this critical stage of post-production that the real magic happens, allowing you to sculpt the image into a reflection of your artistic intent.

As we delve into the tools available for editing, it's essential to recognize the range of options at our disposal. From professional-grade software like Adobe Photoshop and Lightroom to user-friendly apps like Snapseed and VSCO, today's digital landscape is saturated with choices. Each platform brings its own set of features and capabilities, catering to photographers from all walks of life. Learning to navigate these tools can feel overwhelming, but breaking them down into their core functions helps demystify the process.

Adobe Lightroom stands as a cornerstone in the world of photography editing. This software allows photographers to manage and edit large batches of images seamlessly. Its non-destructive editing feature ensures that your original photo remains untouched, providing flexibility to experiment freely. With tools to adjust exposure, contrast, highlights, shadows, and color balance, Lightroom empowers users to bring out the best in their images.

Photoshop, on the other hand, offers a level of control that is unparalleled. While it can be more complex than Lightroom, it is immensely powerful when it comes to detailed adjustments and creative edits. Photoshop allows photographers to manipulate their images in myriad ways—removing distractions, adding elements, or applying artistic filters. The possibilities are endless, and with the right techniques, you can create images that transcend the typical bounds of photography.

Having spent years navigating these software applications, I have encountered both triumphs and failures. Early in my journey, I recall a particular photograph—a fleeting moment I captured of a sunset illuminating a field. The colors were stunning in reality, but upon uploading the photo for editing, I found it lacked the vibrancy I had experienced in person. Determined to salvage the moment, I meticulously adjusted the saturation and contrast in Lightroom. While the final version was indeed more luminous, I learned a valuable lesson: editing should enhance your vision, not reinvent it.

Trial and error is a significant aspect of post-production. Embracing mistakes is crucial for growth. One of my most memorable failures occurred when I became overly reliant on the available filters in Photoshop. In an attempt to simplify my workflow, I quickly dismissed my instinctual understanding of color and texture. The resulting images looked artificial and lacked the authenticity I aimed to convey. It was a pivotal moment that reminded me that each edit should start with purpose and an understanding of the story I wanted to tell.

Experimentation is central to finding your editing style. This process begins with evaluating your artistic vision and considering what emotions you wish to evoke. For instance, some photographers are drawn to vivid, high-contrast images that command attention, while others prefer a softer, muted palette that evokes a sense of nostalgia. Recognizing your preferences will steer your editing process and help you establish a signature style.

As a practical exercise, take time to edit a series of images with varying moods in mind. Select a theme, such as "Serenity" or "Chaos," and capture photos that embody these concepts. Then, in the editing phase, utilize different tools to manipulate the images according to the intended mood. For "Serenity," you might emphasize soft lighting and pastel colors to create an ethereal atmosphere. Conversely, "Chaos" could be expressed through stark contrasts, bold colors, and dynamic cropping. This exercise will not only hone your editing skills but also encourage you to think critically about how your choices in post-production shape the viewer's experience.

The aspect of learning to edit through practice cannot be overstated. In my early days of photography, I often found myself gravitating toward one editing technique—brightness adjustments, for example—without exploring others that could add depth, dimension, and emotion to my images. This narrow focus limited my growth. As I began to experiment with shadows, highlights, and even grain, I found previously unseen textures in my work.

A useful exercise here is to dedicate a week to exploring one editing technique each day. On day one, focus on exposure adjustments; day two, experiment with color grading; day three, delve into cropping and composition, and so on. Each time you shoot, apply what you learned during your experimental phase to your new images, reflecting on how it transforms your work.

One of the most essential aspects of editing is understanding the role of storytelling. While technical excellence is vital, the narrative element breathed into an image can elevate it from a simple photograph to an impactful work of art. When I edited a series of portraits of my grandmother, I aimed not just to present her likeness, but to reveal her spirit. Studying her expressions and the subtle emotions that played across her face, I adjusted the light within the image, softened the shadows, and opted for a nostalgic sepia tone. The result was a photograph that felt rich with history, one that spoke to the stories woven into her life.

Understanding the broader context of editing enhances your effectiveness. Familiarize yourself with the ways different photographers approach the editing process, learning from their techniques while staying true to your voice. Established photographers often share their editing workflows in online tutorials or workshops. Engaging with these resources can provide valuable insights into new styles and strategies you may not have considered.

Social media platforms have also played a significant role in shaping contemporary editing trends. As photographers share their work online, distinct styles can garner attention and influence the aesthetic preferences of audiences. This exposure can be a double-edged sword; while it can inspire creativity, it can also lead to an unhealthy fixation on trying to conform to trends. It's important to discern what resonates with you personally while remaining open to innovation.

Editing isn't just about technical adjustments—it's also about understanding the emotional responses photographs elicit. One of the most profound breakthroughs in my editing journey occurred when I learned to trust my instincts about mood and feeling. There was a photograph I captured in a rain-soaked city after a storm, where the reflections of lights shimmered in puddles. Initially, I brightened the image, thinking it should be vibrant and lively, but the essence felt lost. By darkening the image and enhancing the blues and purples, I discovered a depth that aligned with the melancholy beauty of the moment.

This brings to light the relationship between creativity and emotion in photography. To develop this connection further, I encourage you to engage in a reflective exercise after editing. For each photograph you edit, take a moment to write down the emotions you aim to convey. Reflect on whether your edits are enhancing or detracting from that goal. This practice will ground your editing decisions while fostering a deeper connection to your work.

In addition to traditional software like Lightroom and Photoshop, specialized applications can yield stunning results too. For instance, apps like Aurora HDR make high dynamic range (HDR) editing accessible and approachable, allowing photographers to enhance details in both highlights and shadows seamlessly. Similarly, mobile apps such as VSCO and Snapseed offer robust editing features, allowing photographers to edit directly from their smartphones. Embracing these tools can empower you to create stunning imagery without the need for extensive software knowledge.

Embarking on your editing journey may create new paths you never considered. One of the most exciting aspects of creativity is that it isn't confined to just one medium. If you have a background in digital art, consider integrating those skills into your photographic process. Utilizing layering techniques or mastering digital brushes in Photoshop can create hybrid works that elevate your photography into a new realm of artistry.

Remember, the goal of editing is not merely to increase technical quality but to enhance the narrative of the photograph. The editing room can transform your raw capture into a visual story—one that resonates with both you and your audience. As I reflect on some of my most cherished images, I recognize that the editing process often lent a heightened sense of purpose to my work, transforming ordinary moments into extraordinary narratives.

The key takeaway is that editing is an extension of your creative voice. Your unique perspective, experiences, and emotional journey shape the way you approach each image. With this in mind, embracing the process of trial and error, experimentation, and reflection is paramount. As you develop your post-production skills, you will discover that editing not only aids in refining your photographs but also nourishes your growth as a photographer and storyteller.

Moving forward, challenge yourself to take on new projects with the intent to push your boundaries. Set aside time to delve deeply into your editing process. Don't be afraid to take risks. Your willingness to explore and embrace the unknown will not only enhance your technical skills but deepen your connection with the art of photography itself.

Conclusively, allow the editing phase to be as exciting as the moment of capture. Embrace the tools, learn from your experiences, celebrate your failures, and let your creative spirit flourish. Photography is a continuous journey, and editing serves as the conduit through which you elevate your craft and storytelling. As you become more comfortable with editing, you'll naturally develop your own style. So, don't be afraid to experiment, seek inspiration, and grow in your artistic expression. The world is filled with beauty—and with the right edits, your vision can shine through every frame you capture.

Sharing in the Digital Age

The digital age has transformed the way photographers share their work, offering unprecedented opportunities to showcase their images to a global audience. Social media platforms, photography websites, and online galleries have become integral to a photographer's journey, not just for showcasing their art but also for engaging with a community of fellow creatives and potential clients. In this subchapter, I will explore the significant impact these platforms have had on photography, sharing personal experiences and encompassing both the rewards and the challenges that come with this instant connectivity. Additionally, I will provide practical advice for effectively sharing images and building a robust online portfolio, so readers can navigate the digital landscape with confidence.

Years ago, when I first ventured into digital photography, my interaction with other photographers was confined to local meetups or the occasional workshop. I relied on print galleries and physical exhibitions to showcase my work, which, while fulfilling, limited audience reach and engagement. However, the advent of social media radically changed the game. Platforms like Instagram, Facebook, and dedicated photography sites such as 500px enabled me to share my photos at a moment's notice. No longer did I have to wait for an exhibition to share my latest work; instead, I could post an image and receive feedback within seconds.

I vividly recall the excitement of posting my first images on Instagram. I had spent hours meticulously editing a photo of a sunset I had captured during a weekend trip. As I pressed "share," I felt an adrenaline rush akin to unveiling my work in a gallery. The instant notifications were overwhelming—the likes, comments, and even the first few follows felt like validation of my efforts. This immediate response not only stoked the flames of my passion but also reinforced my belief in the power of sharing my artistic journey.

One of the most significant benefits of sharing images online is the ability to connect with a diverse audience. Photography is inherently subjective; what resonates with one viewer may not stir another. Online platforms provide a space where varying tastes and preferences coexist. This exposure allowed me to receive feedback from not only friends and family but from people all over the world, offering insights that I had never anticipated. I began to understand the preferences of different audiences, and this informed my work in ways I did not expect.

However, along with these benefits come drawbacks, particularly the pressure to conform to trends or follow specific aesthetics to garner attention. In the past, I felt compelled to mimic popular editing styles that dominated my feed, believing that if I adopted the same look, my work would be more widely accepted. Eventually, I realized that while it's essential to stay current, compromising my artistic vision for the sake of popularity was detrimental. I learned that my unique voice is what truly resonates with viewers.

The challenge of constantly curating content also cannot be overlooked. In the early days of my online sharing, I felt the need to post frequently, fearing that if I went silent, I would lose the audience I had painstakingly built. This led to a cycle of pressure to create content rather than focusing on growth and experimentation. It was an important lesson: sharing should not feel like a chore, but rather an organic extension of my photography journey.

As I navigated these challenges, I began to reflect on my own online presence. I realized that purposefully engaging with the photography community had a dual benefit—it fostered connections and sparked new ideas that enhanced my work. I started reaching out to fellow photographers, engaging in thoughtful discussions about techniques, inspirations, and experiences. This reciprocity not only influenced my art but also created valuable relationships within the community.

Beyond engagement, it became crucial to present my work authentically. A portfolio is often the first point of contact for potential clients or collaborators; thus, how it is curated makes an impression. I started thinking critically about how I wanted to be perceived and what message my portfolio conveyed about my style and dedication to photography.

To assist readers in effectively sharing their images and building an online portfolio, I have compiled a set of practical tips that have served me well over my photographic journey.

First and foremost, define your brand. Consider what themes or concepts you want your work to embody. Think about what sets you apart from other photographers. Whether it's your unique style, the subjects you choose, or the emotions you capture, having a clear vision allows you to curate your portfolio cohesively.

Next, choose the right platforms. Not every social media site is suitable for all photographers. While Instagram is fantastic for visual storytelling, platforms like Behance or Flickr cater more specifically to artists looking to showcase their portfolios. Research where your target audience is most active and find your niche.

Maintaining a consistent posting schedule is key to staying relevant and engaged with your audience. However, prioritize quality over quantity. You might find that posting fewer, higher-quality images generates more interest and feedback than flooding your feed with mediocre photos. Ensure that every image you share adds value to your portfolio, reflecting the best of your work.

Engagement is critical, so be proactive in fostering connections. Comment on other photographers' work, participate in photography challenges, or join groups that align with your interests. This not only adds visibility to your profile but also nurtures a sense of community and support among your peers.

When presenting your work, write engaging captions that provide context. Sharing the story behind an image can evoke a deeper connection with your audience. My most successful posts often include a narrative or insight about the moment I captured, making the image more relatable and memorable.

Additionally, take the time to curate your online portfolio thoughtfully. Categorize your work based on themes, styles, or projects. A well-organized portfolio not only showcases your versatility but also allows potential clients to navigate through your work seamlessly. Include not just finished pieces but also behind-the-scenes images that give insight into your process; this transparency can foster trust and appreciation among viewers.

I personally found immense value in seeking feedback from a trusted circle of fellow photographers or mentors. Constructive criticism can illuminate aspects of your work you might overlook. However, it's also essential to develop a discerning eye for feedback. Ultimately, trust your instincts and vision; the right critique will resonate, allowing for growth while staying true to your artistic voice.

As we live in an age where visual content is consumed rapidly, taking the time to analyze analytics provided by social media platforms can reveal valuable insights into your audience's preferences and engagement patterns. Understanding which photos performed well and why aids in honing your style to align more closely with your audience, cultivating a symbiotic relationship that benefits both.

Finally, keep learning. The digital realm is constantly evolving, and so should your skills. Explore the wealth of online resources, tutorials, and courses available at your disposal. This learning not only enhances your technical abilities but also opens you up to new perspectives and techniques that can influence your work dramatically.

Reflecting on my experiences in this digital era continues to remind me of the significance of balance. While sharing my photography online has drastically widened my horizons and introduced me to countless fellow creatives, I have come to understand that a healthy digital presence must be accompanied by authenticity. I've learned to embrace both my uniqueness and the diversity of voices within the photography community.

As you embark on your journey of digital sharing, remember that it is not merely about gaining likes or followers; it is about fostering connections, refining your craft, and sharing your visual stories with the world. Whether through a heartfelt comment on another photographer's post or embarking on a collaborative project, your digital presence should reflect the passion and dedication you hold for your art.

In conclusion, the digital age offers more than just tools for sharing photographs; it provides a pathway to forge connections, broaden horizons, and evolve as an artist. By embracing this opportunity while holding steadfast to your unique vision, you can cultivate a fulfilling relationship with the photography community, share your stories, and continue to grow in a way that resonates with your heart and inspires others along the way. As the world encourages us to see through our individual lenses, remember that your perspective is a powerful part of the collective narrative unfolding within the realm of photography.

CHAPTER 7

PRACTICAL EXERCISES: IGNITE YOUR CREATIVITY

Challenging Your Limits

The world of photography is vast, filled with endless possibilities and avenues for exploration. Yet, often, we tend to find comfort in our routines, sticking to familiar techniques and subjects. While comfort may feel safe, it can stifle growth and creativity. This subchapter is a call to action—to push your boundaries and embrace challenges that will stretch your creative limits and expand your understanding of photography.

Throughout my journey as a photographer, I have encountered numerous moments where I felt stagnant, unsure of how to evolve my craft. It was during one such phase that I decided to undertake a series of challenges designed to provoke growth. These challenges not only re-energized my passion for photography but also provided me with invaluable lessons about my style, approach, and creative potential. These experiences shaped me into a more versatile and intuitive photographer, and I believe they can do the same for you.

In this subchapter, you are invited to take part in various exercises that will encourage experimentation, exploration, and ultimately, growth. Each challenge serves a unique purpose, whether it's to enhance your technical skills, cultivate your eye for composition, or deepen your emotional connection with your subject. As you embark on this journey, remember to maintain an open mind and a playful spirit. Embrace uncertainty and messiness, as these are often the precursors of brilliance.

Challenge 1: The 30-Day Photo Challenge

The very first challenge I undertook as a means to reignite my creative spark was a simple yet effective 30-day photo challenge. Each day, I set out to capture one photograph based on a specific theme or prompt. This discipline forced me to think outside the box and be intentional with my photography.

The prompts varied from "Nature" to "Portrait" to "Street Life." Some days, the themes were broad, and other days they were narrowly focused. For example, on a day designated for "Textures," I had to delve into the intricate details of my surroundings—the roughness of tree bark, the smoothness of a stone surface, or the delicate patterns of fabric. Each prompt tested my ability to interpret and visualize different subjects, while also adhering to the specific theme.

Even when I was not inspired, knowing that I had a daily task helped me to go out and shoot. There were days I felt uninspired or overwhelmed, and yet, forcing myself to answer the call to create led me to surprising moments of beauty and insight. I discovered new angles, experimented with different lenses, and learned to appreciate the small details often overlooked in the chaos of everyday life.

Reflective Prompt: After completing this challenge, take a moment to reflect. What were some of the images you created that surprised you? Did you notice any themes or styles emerging in your work? Consider where you found the most joy and which prompts challenged you the most.

Challenge 2: The "One Lens, One Month" Experiment

In the spirit of encouraging creativity and honing technical skills, the "One Lens, One Month" challenge is another fantastic way to push your limits. The idea is quite simple: for an entire month, commit to using just one lens on your camera. This limitation can be both daunting and liberating, forcing you to adapt and think critically about composition and framing.

I undertook this experiment with a 50mm prime lens, known for its versatility while maintaining a shallow depth of field. In narrowing my options, I was compelled to overcome the urge to switch lenses when encountering challenging situations. Initially, I felt constrained. However, I soon realized that creativity often flourishes in limitations. I began looking for fresh perspectives, shooting from unconventional angles, and making the best of the focal length I was working with.

Throughout the month, I learned to play with depth of field, experimenting with different apertures to evoke various emotions in my photographs. As a prime lens, my 50mm forced me to literally step back or move closer, teaching me about the importance of my physical relationship to my subject. Moreover, I discovered the beauty of simplicity; by focusing on only one lens, my creative voice became clearer, and my eyes were trained to notice significant elements in my compositions.

Reflective Prompt: At the end of the month, examine the collection of images you created. What surprises did you discover about the adaptability of your chosen lens? Did you find new techniques that became essential in your practice? This self-evaluation will help clarify how limitations can serve as creative inspiration.

Challenge 3: The "One Color" Project

Another challenge that proved transformative for me was the "One Color" project—an exercise centered on capturing images all derived from a single color palette. I chose the color blue and went about my days seeking out various shades, tones, and contexts where blue appeared. From the striking blues of the sky to the muted hues of worn-out objects, this project forced me to engage thoughtfully with color as an element of storytelling.

Engaging with a single color heightened my awareness of light and how it interacts with different surfaces. I explored abstraction, revealing the emotional resonance of color in ways I had never considered before. The challenge also became a gateway into developing a unique series of photographs that evoke a mood, making it easier to communicate a visual narrative across a collection.

By the end of the project, I had accumulated a collection showcasing various interpretations of blue—from a desaturated wintry landscape to the rich vibrancy of street art. Each image spoke not only of my thematic choice but also of the connections made through the act of intentional observation.

Reflective Prompt: After this challenge, reflect on how focusing on a single color shifted your perspective. What did you learn about color theory and emotion in photography? Consider how you might approach a different color or vary the parameters of this project in the future.

Challenge 4: Embracing Candid Photography

Candid photography has a magic of its own, capturing real moments as they unfold. However, many photographers, including myself, often shy away from this type due to the inherent unpredictability. To expand my comfort zone, I decided to spend a week dedicated solely to candid photography, whether in bustling streets, public parks, or family gatherings.

During this week, I embraced spontaneity and immersed myself in my surroundings. The objective was to remain unobtrusive, capturing interactions, emotions, and fleeting moments without directing or staging scenes. The beauty of candid photography lies in its authenticity, but it required me to develop keen observational skills.

I found myself becoming more attuned to the nuances of body language, facial expressions, and the subtle dynamics between people. Each photograph told a story—an unexpected encounter between strangers, a child's joy captured mid-laughter, or the contemplative gaze of an elderly person on a park bench. As I reviewed my collection, I was amazed at the depth of emotion conveyed through these unguarded moments.

Reflective Prompt: After a week of candid photography, take time to analyze the emotional weight of your images. What moments resonated with you the most? How did it feel to step back, observe, and capture rather than direct? Reflecting on these experiences can help you find a balance between posed and candid styles in your work.

Challenge 5: 365 Days of Photography

If you're up for an extensive and rigorous challenge, consider embarking on a 365-day photography project. The concept is simple: take a photograph every single day for a year. While daunting, this challenge can radically transform your approach to the medium, instilling discipline and encouraging you to discover beauty in the ordinary.

I began my own 365-day challenge with a mix of excitement and trepidation. The first few weeks felt invigorating, as I explored new places and experimented with techniques. However, as the novelty wore off, it became increasingly difficult to find motivation each day. Yet it was during these lulls that I learned the most about persistence and creativity. Some days, I shot spectacular landscapes, while on others, I simply took detailed snapshots of mundane objects in my home.

The challenge served as a compass for creative exploration. I began to appreciate not just stunning sunsets or memorable trips, but also the quiet poetry found within unremarkable moments. The more I shot, the more I realized that inspiration was everywhere—I merely had to be present and alert.

Reflective Prompt: After completing the 365-day project, look back over the entire set of images. What was your evolution throughout the year? Did certain themes or patterns emerge? Reflect on your growth as a photographer, noting how daily practice has shaped your style and perspective.

Challenge 6: Exhibition Preparation

The final challenge I propose is one that culminates in a tangible outcome: preparing a photography exhibition. While this might feel daunting, it can be one of the most rewarding experiences you embark on. Curating a collection forces you to reflect deeply on your work and conceptualize your artistic vision.

I began my own journey towards hosting an exhibition by selecting a theme that resonated deeply with me. I chose to focus on "Connections," documenting interactions between individuals within urban spaces. The process involved selecting images, deciding on the narrative arc, and considering how to present the work effectively.

Assembling an exhibition required my total commitment—from editing the final images to designing the layout. I spent long hours contemplating how to evoke emotions through arrangement and cohesive storytelling. This challenge taught me substantial lessons about the importance of presentation, the impact of curation on visual narrative, and instilled a sense of pride as I shared my work with an audience.

Reflective Prompt: After your exhibition experience, reflect on how this process affected your perspective on your work. What insights did you gain about your artistic vision through curating? How did presenting your photography shape your understanding of its value?

As you consider diving into these challenges, remember that the real transformation occurs outside the boundaries of comfort. Each challenge is an opportunity for reflection, experimentation, and growth. As you embark on your practice, approach these exercises with curiosity and a willingness to learn from every frame captured.

Ultimately, every challenge completed will lead you closer to discovering your unique voice in photography. Embrace the journey, accept the uncertainties, and let your creativity flourish as you challenge your limits. Whether you discover new techniques, refine your style, or form deeper connections with your subjects, you will emerge a more confident and creative photographer, ready to embrace whatever comes next.

Collaborative Projects

The world of photography, while often perceived as an individual endeavor, is rich with opportunities for collaboration. Engaging with fellow photographers or artists not only broadens our creative horizons but also infuses our work with diverse perspectives that can lead to unexpected and inspiring outcomes. In this subchapter, we will explore the transformative power of collaboration, sharing personal stories and insights, while providing practical exercises aimed at fostering a collaborative spirit in your photographic journey.

One of my most memorable collaborative projects involved a fellow photographer, Sarah, whose approach to visual storytelling was strikingly different from mine. Sarah had a background in documentary photography, while I had spent years honing my skills in fine art portraiture. When we decided to work together on a project that aimed to document the lives of the artisans in our local community, we tapped into our contrasting styles to create a body of work that was richer and more nuanced than anything we could have produced individually.

We began by conducting a series of interviews with the artisans, asking them about their craft, their challenges, and their dreams. This initial phase became a powerful foundation for our collaboration. As Sarah captured the artisans' working environments and the stories behind their creations, I focused on the intimate aspects of their expressions and emotions during our conversations. Our different approaches to photography complemented each other beautifully, leading to a series of images that not only showcased the artisans' skills but also conveyed their passion and commitment.

The process was not without its challenges. At times, we found ourselves butting heads over creative decisions. Sarah was inclined to capture images in a documentary style, emphasizing realism and context, while I was drawn to compositional techniques that highlighted the beauty of form and color. These conflicts, however, ultimately fueled our growth as artists. By discussing our differing visions, we deepened our understanding of each other's perspectives and pushed one another to explore new ideas. When we presented the final series at a local gallery, the feedback was overwhelmingly positive, with viewers noting how the fusion of our styles created a compelling narrative that resonated on multiple levels.

This experience reinforced for me the idea that collaboration is not merely about combining efforts; it is also about engaging in a dialogue that challenges our assumptions and perceptions. Timidity can stifle creativity, but collaboration can ignite it by encouraging us to step outside our comfort zones. In working with Sarah, I learned to appreciate the elegance of simplicity that often defines documentary photography, while she gained insights into the emotional resonance of carefully composed portraits. As a result, both our practices evolved in unexpected ways.

To harness the power of collaboration in your own work, consider practical exercises that can lead to impactful partnerships. Start by reflecting on your artistic goals and identifying areas in which collaboration could prove beneficial. Ask yourself: What aspects of your work do you feel could be enriched by another perspective? Perhaps you seek to explore a theme that resonates with multiple mediums or want to push the boundaries of your current style. Recognizing these goals will help you find the right collaborators who can complement your vision.

One way to initiate collaborative projects is through informal meetups or workshops with fellow photographers and artists in your area. Create a list of local art communities, photography clubs, or even online forums where you can connect with like-minded individuals. Approach these gatherings with an open mind, willing to share your ideas and, more importantly, to listen. Engage in conversations that explore each member's artistic journey, struggles, and aspirations. This exchange of stories can seed collaborative ideas that may lead to projects rich in content and perspective.

As you form connections, consider embarking on a joint project that allows each collaborator to leverage their strengths. Create a small group to tackle a thematic photography challenge. For example, each participant could interpret the theme of "resilience"—an exploration of how individuals or communities overcome adversity—through their own lens. Allow each member the freedom to interpret the subject in their unique style while committing to a shared outcome. This approach fosters a sense of cohesiveness and allows for self-expression, all while benefiting from the creative input of others.

In another collaborative exercise, introduce an element of surprise by utilizing a "photographer's exchange." In this activity, each participant (or pair) is assigned a photography scenario that they must interpret through their distinct styles, but there's a twist: you'll only be able to see the result after the project is completed. For instance, one photographer may be tasked with capturing intimate portraits in a bustling market, while another explores landscapes during the golden hour. The exchange can yield delightful surprises as each artist discovers how their unique interpretations can converge or diverge in unexpected ways.

Documenting the journey of collaboration is equally valuable. Keep journals to chronicle your thoughts, emotions, and discoveries throughout the process, and reference these reflections when discussing your collaborative results with your partner. Engaging in open dialogue about your experiences will not only deepen your connection with your collaborator but foster a greater understanding of the dynamics of your artistic process. Over time, you may discover patterns and themes in your work that reflect your collaborative spirit, leading to future projects shaped by your reflective practices.

One collaboration that particularly stands out involved working with a local dancer who was eager to interpret her movements through a visual medium. Our project aimed to capture the dance in urban spaces, connecting the fluidity of her art with the often rigid environments around us. The goal was to explore the contrast between movement and architecture, a theme that both of us were excited to bring to life.

The initial planning sessions were filled with brainstorming ideas, scouting locations, and discussing how best to express the connection between dance and the urban landscape. I quickly learned that what I envisioned for the project was very different from the reality of shooting with a live dancer in motion. Relying heavily on spontaneous captures proved to be invaluable, as some of my most striking images came from abstracted moments where the dancer seemed to vanish into the surrounding environment. We discovered that the dance was indeed about the interaction with its surroundings, and my perspective on urban photography evolved as a result.

Once again, our differing approaches played a key role in the final product. She brought her knowledge of movement and choreography, compelling me to consider how concepts of rhythm and timing could influence my compositions. We both engaged in a process of experimentation where the rhythm of her movements spurred my camera's shutter. The interplay of light, shadow, and fluid motion resulted in images that felt alive—a dance captured in time.

This collaboration fostered my appreciation for the art of movement and solidified the notion that creativity thrives in shared pursuits. Taking part in this project encouraged me to seek out collaborative opportunities that would not only resonate with my current work but would challenge me to see the world in new ways— ways I would have never approached had I chosen to work alone.

As you explore the potential of collaboration, remember that the most fruitful partnerships often arise from an environment of trust and open communication. Be transparent about your creative goals and expectations right from the outset. Clarifying your vision ensures that all collaborators are aligned in their endeavors, ultimately resulting in a cohesive and fulfilling creative process.

Another exercise to consider is embarking on an artist residency or creative retreat that emphasizes collaboration. These environments foster collective brainstorming and creative synergy, allowing you to immerse yourself in new perspectives while working alongside artists from diverse backgrounds. Plus, the structured timeframe can add an exciting layer of urgency to the projects. I once participated in a retreat focused on visual storytelling, where we spent a weekend creating a community narrative. Each photographer was responsible for interpreting a different facet of life in the area, from the mundane to the extraordinary. We shared our work at the end of the retreat, and the final visual narrative showcased the rich tapestry of experiences and perspectives of the location.

In conclusion, embracing collaboration as an integral part of your photographic journey can enhance your creativity in ways you may not have anticipated. By working alongside other artists, you can expand your understanding of art, challenge your creative boundaries, and cultivate a deeper appreciation for the diverse perspectives that exist within the realm of visual storytelling.

Through collaborative projects, we share not just images but stories that intertwine our experiences and visions. Each collaborative endeavor not only enriches our individual practices but also contributes to a vibrant community of artists willing to share their explorations, joys, and creative discoveries.

So, step out of your comfort zone, seek out fellow photographers and artists, and embark on collaborative projects that allow you to weave together the threads of your unique visions. The result? A tapestry of creativity that transcends the individual, inspiring those who witness your collective artistry.

As you take these steps, always keep in mind: in collaboration, the possibilities are boundless. The next innovative project could be just a conversation away, waiting to unfold into a beautiful exploration that reflects not only your artistry but the essence of the connections forged along the way.

Documenting a Day in Your Life

The sun peeked through my curtains, casting warm golden rays that danced across my room. I grabbed my camera from the nightstand, feeling an invigorating thrill of anticipation wash over me. Today, I would document an entire day of my life through the lens— every moment, every detail, every mundane task transformed into a frame of beauty. This exercise was more than just capturing images; it was an exploration, an invitation to slow down and truly see the world around me.

As I prepared for the day, I reflected on the theme that would guide my photographic journey. Themes can anchor a project, bringing coherence and depth to the collection. Personally, I find that choosing a theme helps to heighten my awareness and focus during the narrative-building process. For this exercise, I decided to embrace the theme of "Routine and Ritual," showcasing the small yet significant moments that usually slip beneath the surface of daily life.

With my theme in mind, I moved into the kitchen for breakfast. The soft light poured in, illuminating the simple act of pouring milk over my cereal. I paused, raising my camera to capture the swirl of white cascading into the bowl, the textures of the cereal contrasting against the smoothness of the milk. I framed the shot at an angle that highlighted both the milk and the bowl, creating a visual story about nourishment. This was not just another breakfast—this was a moment of sustenance and care, an act of love towards myself.

After breakfast, my routine continued uninterrupted. I slipped into my shoes and ventured outside for a brief walk. The world buzzed with activity. I noticed details I often overlooked: the intricate patterns of dew drops clinging to blades of grass, the soft rustling of leaves in the gentle breeze, and the way a child's laughter echoed in the distance, blending seamlessly with the chirps of birds. Armed with my camera, I wanted to capture the intimacy of these moments.

I focused on the dew-laden grass and crouched low, angling my camera to emphasize the droplets shimmering like jewels. I played with depth of field, blurring the background to draw attention to those tiny crystals of nature. Each click of the shutter emphasized my intention to see and document life in its simplest form. How often do we overlook such beauty? Through this exercise, I sought to remind myself—and, ideally, others—that remarkable moments are often hidden within the everyday.

As the day progressed, my camera became an extension of my perception. I moved on to my next task: tidying up my living space. This was more than just cleaning; it was part of my ritual—an act that brought clarity and a sense of accomplishment. While organizing, I captured shots of ordinary items in new ways. The stark shadows cast by a vase on the wall became a study in contrast, and the texture of the books lining my shelves told stories of knowledge and imagination.

At midday, I prepared lunch, which offered another opportunity to observe the rhythm of my routine. As I sliced vegetables for a fresh salad, I focused on the vibrant colors: the deep crimson of tomatoes, the crisp green of lettuce, and the sunny yellow of bell peppers. Each slice produced a soft crunch that resonated as I captured the essence of food—which, in many cultures, acts as a connection to community and celebration. With my camera poised, I framed an overhead shot that showcased the beauty of the ingredients, allowing the colors to pop against the textured surface of the cutting board.

Throughout the day, I discovered that the act of documenting my life was similar to meditation. It invited me to step outside of my internal dialogue and immerse myself in the present moment. Every click of the shutter became an affirmation of existence, a conscious acknowledgment of the surrounding world. Yet, it also compelled me to think critically about how I composed each shot. What was the story I wanted to tell? What elements contributed to that narrative?

As afternoon light began to soften and shift, I decided to capture moments of rest. I settled into my favorite reading nook with a book I had long wanted to explore. A warm cup of tea accompanied me, steam curling elegantly into the air. Here, the light filtered through the window, casting a gentle glow that wrapped around me like a comforting embrace. I positioned my camera to capture not only the book but also the inviting atmosphere that had formed in this personal sanctuary. The intimate setting inspired a quiet reflection on how vital it is to carve out spaces for ourselves amidst the hustle of life.

With evening approaching, I ventured outside once more, this time to witness the transformation that occurred as day turned to dusk. Golden hour bathed everything in a warm hue, and I took my time to relish the fading light. The streets felt alive; the magic of twilight united neighbors, drawing them out of their homes like moths to a flame. I aimed my camera at the kids riding their bikes down the street, their laughter mingling with the soft rustle of leaves—this was where joy thrived, wrapped in the fabric of daily life.

Encouraged by the connection I felt with my surroundings, I turned my lens toward the sunset. The colors shifted fluidly from brilliant orange to shades of lavender and indigo, creating a kaleidoscope that was nothing short of extraordinary. Shooting against the horizon, I framed silhouettes of trees, encapsulating the calm that dusk brought. This was a reminder that beauty often lies at the boundary of day and night—a sentiment that echoes in our own lives.

As the sky darkened, I returned home to reflect on the images I had captured throughout the day. I connected with my artistic intentions, thinking about how the moments, slices of life I documented, aligned with my original theme of "Routine and Ritual." Each photograph conveyed a sense of storytelling, vibrantly illustrating how simple acts influenced my day and brought a greater sense of purpose.

In the quiet of the evening, I sat with my digital slideshow—an assemblage of these everyday moments that turned into a tapestry composed of color, emotion, and insight. I began the process of editing, where each image transformed into a conversation piece that spoke not just of what I saw, but of how I felt. I learned that the beauty in this exercise lies in the act of selection; it allowed me to curate my experiences, to relive those moments, and to appreciate each one for its unique story.

When viewing the collection as a whole, I was reminded that everyday life, often perceived as mundane, is filled with layers of significance. It is a testament to the power of observation, of taking the time to notice what we might otherwise let slip away. As you embark on your own day of documenting life, I encourage you to embrace the mundane with open arms.

Think about the themes that speak to you—today, tomorrow, or in your everyday life. Let them guide your lens as you navigate through familiar spaces. Consider how light shifts throughout the day, permanently altering the fabric of your images. Find inspiration in the smallest details, for therein lies the heart of your story.

When you sit down to reflect on your collection, ask yourself: What moments moved you? How did your perspective shift by just bringing your camera into the fold? What narratives began to emerge from the snapshots of your routine?

As you strive to capture a day in your life, remember that no moment is too small to be appreciated and documented. In embracing even the dullest of routines, you may uncover the richness of everyday life. Over time, this exercise can become a practice of gratitude, deepening your connection to your surroundings and profoundly influencing your artistry.

To assist you in this journey, I encourage you to prepare with a few guidelines in mind:

1. **Choose a Theme:** Consider what resonates with you. Themes such as 'Connection,' 'Change,' or 'Silence' can effectively guide your narrative.

2. **Plan Your Day:** Think about the elements of your daily routines that you want to capture. Make a rough curative plan but remain open to spontaneity.

3. **Frame with Intention:** As you shoot, ask yourself what you want each image to convey and how you can enhance that through framing and composition.

4. **Embrace the Ordinary:** Look at common tasks through a new lens. Mundane moments can reveal extraordinary stories.

5. **Reflect on Your Experience:** At the end of your day, spend some time going through your images and share them—whether in a book, a blog, or simply with friends. Let the stories unfold.

In documenting a full day, you are not just recording moments on a timeline; you are weaving together a narrative that reflects who you are and how you exist in the world. Without a doubt, performance art meets life in this captivating exercise, offering opportunities for creativity, reflection, and joy. Embrace it fully, and you will discover not just the beauty of captured moments, but also the art of seeing life in all its forms. Through this practice, you may ultimately find not just artistic growth, but a deeper connection to your own life story—one frame at a time.

CHAPTER 8

THE PHILOSOPHY OF SEEING

Mindfulness in Photography

In the fast-paced world we live in, it can be easy to overlook the subtle beauty around us. The hustle and bustle of daily life often distracts us from the nuances that make our environments unique, vibrant, and worthy of capturing through the lens. As photographers, we have the unique opportunity to freeze moments in time, but it requires more than technical skill—it demands a mindful approach to seeing and experiencing the world.

Mindfulness in photography is about cultivating a state of awareness that allows us to engage deeply with our surroundings. It encourages us to slow down, to be fully present in the moment, and to observe the intricacies of life that often go unnoticed. When we practice mindfulness, we begin to appreciate not just what we see, but how we feel in that moment, how the light dances across a subject, or how a fleeting expression can encapsulate the depth of human experience.

I vividly remember the first time I came across the concept of mindfulness in photography. I was attending a workshop led by a seasoned photographer who had a reputation for capturing heartfelt moments with an uncanny sense of intuition. During one of the sessions, he encouraged us to leave our cameras behind for a brief period and simply observe our surroundings. We were to find a spot— any spot—and immerse ourselves in the sensory experience of that place. What did we see? What did we hear? What emotions did we feel?

At first, I found it challenging. My mind raced with the images I could capture, the compositions waiting to be framed, and the technical settings I would adjust to get the perfect shot. Yet, as I settled into the exercise, I began to let go of those distractions. I noticed the gentle rustling of leaves, the distant laughter of children playing, the colors of the sky shifting as daylight waned. I found beauty in the ordinary moments—the shadows cast by an old tree, the delicate petals of a flower swaying in the breeze, the way the sunset transformed the landscape into a canvas of warmth.

Returning to my camera after that experience was a revelation. The photographs I took afterward felt richer, more layered in meaning. The mindful practice had opened up my creative vision and deepened my understanding of what I wanted to convey in my work. I realized that photography is not merely about capturing images; it is an art form that thrives on connection and presence.

To cultivate mindfulness in photography, one needs to develop a practice that integrates the principles of being present and observing intentionally. Here are some exercises to help you strengthen this practice in your photographic journey.

The first exercise is simple yet profound: take a walk without your camera. Choose a familiar route, perhaps a path you take every day, but without the intention of photographing anything. As you walk, focus on each step, notice how your feet connect to the ground, and be aware of the rhythm of your breath. Allow yourself to become fully immersed in the experience of walking. What do you feel? What aromas waft through the air? What sights capture your attention?

As you engage your senses, pay particular attention to what typically goes unnoticed. The texture of the bark on a tree, the patterns in the clouds, or even the play of light and shadow across your path can ignite a sense of wonder and curiosity. By discovering the details of your environment, you will likely find inspiration for future photographic endeavors.

Next, practice the "60-Second Rule." When you arrive at a location, spend the first minute simply observing before picking up your camera. Use this time to scan your surroundings, but don't just look—truly see. What emotions arise? After one minute, choose one subject that draws you in—this could be an object, a person, or a scene. Spend another minute observing that subject. How does it exist within its environment? What emotions does it evoke? How would you frame it?

This exercise encourages you to develop a deeper connection not only with your subjects but also with the act of observing itself. These moments of contemplation will help ground your mind, allowing you to approach your camera with a renewed sense of purpose.

Another effective way to incorporate mindfulness into your photography is through breathwork. The next time you set out to shoot, take a few moments to ground yourself through focused breathing. Find a comfortable position, close your eyes, and take several deep breaths—inhale deeply through your nose, hold it for a brief moment, and exhale slowly through your mouth. Allow your thoughts to settle and your busy mind to quiet.

Once you feel centered, open your eyes and step into the world full of potential. With each photograph, approach your subject with an awareness rooted in your steady breathing. Notice how your breath syncs with the flow of your surroundings. This practice helps to maintain a calm demeanor and encourages you to become an observer of the moment, increasing your ability to capture images that resonate.

Mindfulness also extends to the way we engage with our subjects. Whether you're photographing strangers on the street or close friends, it is essential to establish a connection before raising your camera. Strike up a conversation; ask them about their story or how they feel about being photographed. By taking the time to engage with your subject, you foster an emotional connection that translates into authenticity in your images.

I recall a memorable portrait session with a woman I originally met during a charity event. Her name was Lucy, and she was sharing her journey through mental health awareness. I approached her, camera in hand, but before I began snapping away, I felt it necessary to understand her story. As I listened to her experiences, I could feel a shift in the atmosphere; the walls she had built began to fade. I captured images of her laughter, her vulnerability, and her fierce determination.

The portraits my camera produced were not merely photographs; they encapsulated an emotional story because I chose to be present in that moment. Mindfully connecting with my subject allowed me to create images that resonated profoundly, sparking conversation and reflection in others.

Moreover, the practice of mindfulness in photography is not limited to people. When working with landscapes or still life, it's essential to explore the relationship between subject and environment. Take a moment to observe the interplay of light and shadow. How does the light bathe the scene? What colors emerge? What emotions arise when you see the landscape before you?

One of my favorite moments capturing a sunset exemplified this perfectly. As I arrived at my chosen location, the sky began to shift with hues of orange, pink, and indigo. Instead of hastily setting my camera, I paused, allowing the serene beauty to wash over me. I breathed in the salt from the nearby ocean and listened to the gentle waves lapping at the shore.

Once I felt grounded and focused, I took my camera and began to frame my shots, yet my mind retained that quiet, peaceful awareness. I captured the soft brushstrokes of light across the water's surface, the silhouettes of seagulls flying by, and the distant mountains fading into the twilight. Every shot I took emanated a sense of tranquility that I felt in that moment, reinforcing the importance of anchoring oneself in the experience of photography.

As we delve deeper into the interplay between mindfulness and photography, we can explore the concept of intentionality. Every photograph we take should have a purpose or meaning behind it. Before taking a shot, ask yourself: What do I want to convey? How will this image affect the viewer? This intentional approach encourages mindfulness in both composition and subject matter.

When photographing street scenes, for example, it's easy to get caught up in shooting everything in sight. However, by intentionally selecting your subjects and framing your shots with purpose, you can foster deeper storytelling within your work. Take a moment to analyze the details—what person, interaction, or moment feels compelling?

In my street photography, I've learned the importance of waiting for the right moment to unfold, rather than snapping aimlessly. I once found myself in a bustling market where vendors hawked their colorful wares. Instead of rushing from stall to stall, I lingered. Suddenly, a child wandered into the frame, joyfully playing with a balloon while two elderly women exchanged stories nearby. I carefully captured that scene, and the resulting image spoke volumes about joy, connection, and the flow of life amidst the chaos.

Practicing mindfulness in photography not only enhances our vision but also fosters resilience. The creative process is often filled with challenges and frustrations, and it's easy to become disheartened by mistakes or setbacks. Yet, when we adopt a mindful approach, we cultivate a sense of patience and understanding that allows us to embrace our imperfections.

When exploring new techniques or experimenting with unfamiliar settings, take each opportunity as a learning experience. If a shot doesn't turn out the way you envisioned, rather than succumbing to disappointment, observe what went wrong with curiosity. Gentle self-reflection allows us to grow and adapt, ultimately refining our craft over time.

Embracing mindfulness also involves acknowledging the emotional impact of our images. Every photograph tells a story, whether consciously or subconsciously. Therefore, be mindful of the emotions you wish to convey in your work; if you aim to capture a joyful moment, allow that joy to emanate through your compositions. If it's somber or reflective, embrace the quiet beauty in those feelings.

In conclusion, mindfulness in photography is an invaluable practice for anyone looking to enhance their artistic vision. By slowing down and being present in the moment, we cultivate a deeper awareness that enriches our understanding of the world and influences our photographic outcomes.

Through exercises such as mindful observation, breathwork, intentional engagement with subjects, and a focus on emotional resonance, we learn to connect more profoundly with ourselves and the moments we capture. Mindfulness transforms our photographs into authentic representations of life, encapsulating not only what we see but also how we feel in those fleeting moments.

As you embark on your own photographic journey, I encourage you to infuse mindfulness into your practice. Let the beauty of your surroundings unfurl before you, breathe deeply, listen closely, and relish every moment captured through your lens. Through this mindful approach to photography, you will not only create striking visuals but also discover profound connections to the world around you, breathing new life into your artistic endeavors.

Seeing Beyond the Surface

To truly capture the essence of a moment, a photographer must cultivate the ability to see beyond the surface. Photography, at its core, is more than just pressing a button; it's about observing the world through a lens that distills reality into emotion, narrative, and meaning. As we walk through our daily lives, we are often bombarded by the familiar and the mundane, but hidden within these experiences are stories waiting to be told. Our task as photographers is to peel back the layers of superficiality and truly engage with our surroundings.

Keen observation is the cornerstone of compelling photography. It allows us to uncover the subtle nuances of life that might otherwise go unnoticed. Every scene has a multitude of perspectives, and the ability to explore these perspectives is what transforms a simple photograph into a powerful narrative. A photograph does not merely represent what is seen; it holds the potential to convey feelings, provoke thoughts, and spark connections. This chapter invites you to shift your gaze, encouraging you to look past the first impressions and explore the depths of moments that often escape casual observation.

Consider the difference between seeing and looking. Looking is a passive action; it is often done hurriedly and without deep engagement. Seeing, on the other hand, requires a conscious effort to connect with what lies before you. It involves slowing down and immersing yourself in your environment. This practice invites you to engage all your senses and to be present in the moment, forging a deeper connection with your subjects.

Reflect back on a photograph you've taken that resonates with you. What drew you to that particular scene? What emotions did the moment evoke? It's essential to remember that the subjects of our photographs—the people, places, and objects—have their own stories. While the surface may appear ordinary, each element contains a wealth of history and intimacy. It is your job to uncover those stories, transforming them into impactful visual narratives.

Think of a time when you captured an image that seemed ordinary at first glance. Perhaps it was a bustling street scene or a candid moment with friends. Now, reflect on the emotions that swirled around that image. Did you capture laughter, urgency, tranquility, or chaos? By digging deeper into your experience, you may realize that your photograph encompasses far more than what is physically present in the frame.

One of the most profound lessons I have learned in my photographic journey is the power of patience. I recall a particularly busy market where life bustled around me with vibrant colors and loud noises. As I stood there, camera poised, it was easy to get swept up in the chaos of the moment. However, knowing that real life lay beneath the surface, I decided to take a step back, both physically and mentally. I observed the people interacting, connecting, and engaging with one another.

It was in those moments of stillness that stories began to unfold before my eyes. I noticed the elderly vendor sharing a quiet laugh with a child, the intricate details of produce lined up on tables, and the interplay of light and shadow as the sun descended. Each captured frame told a deeper story, revealing connections among individuals and the atmosphere of the market itself. The underlying heartbeat of the community came alive, and I was able to document that intimacy through my lens.

Additionally, our own emotional states can impact our perception of a scene. When we approach a photograph with preconceived notions, we may inadvertently overlook elements that could offer rich storytelling opportunities. Reflect on your moods and mindsets during your shoots; they can color your perception and the resulting images. A moment of joy may encourage you to seek out smiles and laughter, while feelings of melancholy might lead you to explore loneliness or isolation.

To develop a more profound sense of observation, consider setting aside specific times for exploration. Rather than embarking on a shoot with a specific goal in mind, venture out with the intent to observe. This practice encourages you to be curious about your environment and to immerse yourself in the moment. Try exploring neighborhoods, markets, or parks you haven't visited before, allowing yourself to be guided by what captures your attention.

As you explore, engage in reflective prompts. Ask yourself questions such as: What draws my eye to this particular scene? How do the elements within the frame interact? What emotions do I feel as I observe? How do the colors, textures, and shapes contribute to the overall mood? These questions will help you dig deeper and guide your eye toward all the layers present in any given situation.

An excellent exercise to cultivate your observation skills is to practice "blind shooting." This is defined as photographing without looking through your camera's viewfinder or screen. Choose a subject, close your eyes, and let your instincts guide you. Focus on the sounds, textures, and sensations around you. Afterward, review your images. The result may vary in terms of composition and focus, but the exercise encourages you to break free from traditional constraints and embrace spontaneity.

Interactions with people can also deepen our understanding of the stories we wish to tell. Approach strangers with curiosity, asking them about their lives or situations when appropriate. Listen actively to their stories; this intimate connection can foster greater empathy and enable you to capture their experiences in a way that resonates with authenticity.

There was a moment in my photographic journey that encapsulated this beautifully. While photographing a local café, I noticed a woman sitting alone, her fingers gently tracing the rim of her cup as she gazed out the window. Instead of quickly capturing the scene, I approached her and struck up a conversation. Through our exchange, I discovered she had lost a dear friend recently and was waiting for a letter from her family. Her narrative transformed my initial impression of a solitary moment into something profound and full of emotion. That simple cup of coffee held a deeper narrative, one that influenced how I captured her image. It became a potent symbol of grief, connection, and resilience.

These moments of authentic interaction enrich our photographic stories and foster a deeper connection with our subjects. They challenge us to surrender our preconceived notions and engage with people on a human level. To see beyond the surface is to embrace the vulnerable intricacies that make life beautiful, reminding us that every person we encounter carries a universe of stories within them.

In creating images that reflect this level of observation, we also challenge ourselves to express our unique vision. The perspective we bring to our photography shapes how we convey messages through light, composition, and subject matter. Each photograph tells a part of our story as much as it does the story of the subjects we capture.

As you continue your journey as a photographer, remembering this intrinsic connection is vital. The essence of your images lies in your ability to translate what you see into visual narratives that resonate with others. This becomes particularly significant when curating a body of work or a series. The richness in storytelling often emerges when we allow a multitude of perspectives to intersect and inform one another.

Reflect on the themes that resonate most with you. How can you find ways to visually articulate those themes through your photographs? Perhaps you're drawn to the fleeting moments of joy found in everyday life, the weight of solitude, or the vibrancy of community. Identifying these themes creates a roadmap for your exploration, encouraging a deeper investigation of the world around you.

Another way to enhance your observation skills is to engage in "visual journaling." This involves formulating a series of photographs that explore a common theme over time. Document your observations daily, capturing images that align with your chosen subject matter. The repetitive practice will hone your ability to see nuances you may have previously overlooked and will help articulate your vision more clearly.

As you embark on this exploration, embrace the questions that arise within you. Photography isn't solely about answering questions; it is equally about raising them. Why do certain things catch your eye? What emotions are evoked in response to your surroundings? How do these feelings manifest in your photographs?

This journey of looking beyond the surface is not a destination but a continuous exploration. The more we practice, the more we learn to cultivate a mindset of curiosity and sensitivity. The difference between the ordinary snapshot and a powerful photograph often lies in the photographer's ability to investigate, to peel back layers, and to recognize the stories that reside beneath the surface.

Take a moment to reassess the photographs you've captured thus far. Which images reveal depth beyond what is seen at first glance? What thoughts, feelings, or narratives lie hidden in those frames? These reflections will encourage you to challenge yourself consistently, growing as photographers who can appreciate and translate the rich fabric of life into images.

As we draw this chapter to a close, consider this: photography is a dialogue between the photographer and the world. It is an invitation to engage, to be vulnerable, and to observe the intimate interplay of light, emotion, and time. The process of seeing beyond the surface transforms how we approach our craft, enabling us to capture not just images but the very essence of life itself.

By adopting a mindset of mindfulness and intentional observation, you are more likely to uncover the stories that await—hidden treasures within ordinary moments. Embrace the journey, remain inquisitive, and let your lens take you deeper into the beautiful and complex narratives that surround you. Each frame has the potential to echo the depth of human experience, ultimately connecting us to the universal themes that bind us all together.

Developing a Unique Vision

In the world of photography, developing a unique vision is akin to discovering a hidden treasure within yourself. Each of us carries a distinct set of experiences, perceptions, and emotions that inform our view of the world. This subchapter is an exploration of how those personal nuances can be woven into a photographic narrative that is unapologetically yours.

When I first picked up a camera, I didn't fully grasp the weight of the decision I was making. Sure, I was drawn to the allure of capturing images, freezing moments in time, and telling stories, but I had no idea how deeply this endeavor would influence my identity. A camera, after all, is merely a tool; it is the spirit you breathe into it that transforms it into an extension of yourself. In my quest for a unique vision, I learned that it wasn't about the technical specifications of my camera or the latest editing techniques; it was about unearthing my voice and letting my life experiences guide my lens.

Let us begin by understanding the significance of reflection in the journey to finding your photographic voice. Reflection allows us to step back and analyze our experiences, emotions, and the influences that shape us. It is in identifying the sources of our passion that we can begin to articulate what matters to us in our photography.

Throughout my own growth as a photographer, I found that my unique vision developed from a confluence of personal experiences. For instance, my childhood memories often influence my style. Growing up in a rural village, surrounded by nature, outdoor scenes became my initial playground for creativity. I remember vividly lying in the grass, gazing up at the trees, marveling at the patterns created by dappled sunlight. It was there that my fascination with light and its interplay with the environment began to take root. Those early influences still echo through my work today, as I tend to gravitate toward themes of nature and the emotional connection one can feel within it.

The best photographers are keen observers of their surroundings, and this observation is invariably colored by their life experiences. Explore your upbringing, your family dynamics, your cultural background, and your geographic location. Every aspect has the potential to inform your eye and alter your perspective. Ask yourself: What experiences have shaped how I see the world? Have there been mentors, artists, or moments that ignited my passion for photography? To answer these questions, I encourage you to create a reflective journal. Spend some time documenting significant events, memories, and emotions that resonate with you. This exercise will uncover common threads that can anchor your unique vision and style.

A pivotal element of developing your photographic vision is experimentation. In a society that thrives on instant gratification and social validation, patience can be hard to come by. However, true artistry requires exploration and a willingness to try new things without the weight of judgment. I recall a period in my journey when I felt stifled by the notion of what "good photography" should look like. I realized I was adhering more to the trends than to my individuality. One day, however, I decided to embark on a project that challenged me to step outside those confines. I set a challenge for myself to capture one photograph each day that represented a color, texture, or feeling that spoke to me.

In practicing this daily ritual, I let go of the fear of judgment and embraced spontaneity. I captured autumn leaves in vibrant hues, rusty fences adorned with wildflowers, and even reflections in puddles after a rainstorm. The results were enlightening; these images became visual representations of my emotional state, showing elements of who I am and how I engage with the world. It was an unfiltered expression that led me to appreciate quirks in my style.

In nurturing your unique photographic vision, developing a specific style is crucial. Style is the voice of your vision—it communicates your essence without the need for words. But how does one go about establishing a personal style? Start by analyzing the images that resonate with you. Collect photographs that evoke strong emotional responses, and take note of what they have in common. This could involve analyzing everything from composition to color palettes to subject matter. Understanding these elements helps you refine your style.

As you immerse yourself in this analysis, don't shy away from what feels authentic to you, even if it is different from the mainstream. One of my closest friends, an exceptionally talented photographer, captures urban decay. While this seemingly grim subject matter could be overlooked by many, she finds beauty in abandoned buildings, peeling paint, and echoing silence. Through her perspective, she captures not just images but stories of resilience and history from these forgotten places. Her unique vision stems from her personal fascination with the theme. By recognizing what fuels your creativity, you're already on a path toward establishing your style.

Alongside personal experiences and reflections, the act of storytelling is a cornerstone of delivering your unique vision. Photography is not just about documenting what you see; it's about communicating narratives that evoke emotion and connect with your audience. Engaging with stories helps you curate a selection of images that work together. Each image can become part of a larger dialogue captured through your lens.

Consider this: Have you ever been moved by a photograph solely because of the story attached to it? Perhaps it was a portrait of an elderly man, the deep lines etched on his face telling tales of joy, sorrow, and resilience. Or it could have been an image of a child laughing joyfully, encapsulating the essence of innocence. By intertwining storytelling within your photography, you invite viewers to become part of the narrative.

To practice storytelling, I encourage you to embark on a personal project. This could involve creating a narrative around a specific theme, emotion, or subject that resonates with you. Spend time capturing images that align with your vision, aiming to present a cohesive narrative. Once you have a series of photographs, explore how they interact. Are there images that disrupt the flow? Are there additional pieces that could enhance the storytelling? This exploration will not only help you refine your photography but also unveil a unique narrative thread that represents your voice.

Moreover, let us not overlook the significance of community in shaping your unique vision. Engaging with fellow photographers, attending workshops, and joining photography groups can foster an environment ripe for inspiration and growth. Within a nurturing community, you gain exposure to diverse perspectives, techniques, and styles that can ignite your creativity and challenge your preconceived notions. Participate in critiques, share your work, and be open to feedback, absorbing constructive criticisms.

In my own experience, I've learned that vulnerability can lead to authenticity. When I first started sharing my portfolio at local photography meetups, my heart raced with anxiety. However, I found that vulnerability cultivated connections among fellow artists who resonated with my narrative. Conversations about artistry, successes, and challenges fed my creative wellspring and encouraged me to delve deeper into my own vision. So, find your tribe; it can be a vital catalyst for your growth.

As you embark on this journey of developing a unique photographic vision, I'd like to offer a few practical exercises to foster that growth. These exercises aim to promote reflection, experimentation, and community engagement—key components in your creative evolution.

1. **Reflective Journaling**:

Set aside time each week to reflect on your photography experiences. Write about what inspired you, what you captured, and how you felt emotionally in that moment. Keep a record of your growth and evolving preferences. Perhaps explore themes or subjects that intrigue you. Over time, you'll identify patterns and inspirations that can shape your unique vision.

2. **The Portfolio Project**:

Create three specific portfolios that reflect your style. Curate a collection of 10 images for each portfolio, focusing on different themes or approaches. This could involve a series on nature, urban landscapes, or candid portraits. Once completed, share them with friends or fellow photographers, inviting feedback about the narratives they perceive.

3. **Experiment with Storytelling**:

Choose a single story to communicate through photography over the course of a week. It could be a personal journey, a family tradition, or even a chosen theme like "joy." Capture a series of images that convey this story, aiming to evoke specific emotions. Once complete, narrate the story behind the images, showcasing how they interconnect and articulate your voice.

4. **Engage with the Community**:

Attend local photography meetups or join online photography groups. Share your work, engage in critiques, and explore other artists' creations. Embrace the inspirations that arise from collaborative discussions and collective storytelling. Take note of how the experience shapes your vision.

5. **Rediscover the Ordinary**:

For one week, commit to photographing the mundane aspects of your day—your morning routine, the view from your window, or the coffee shop on the corner. Challenge yourself to find beauty and significance in the ordinary. By honing your observational skills, you'll deepen your connection to your surroundings and uncover layers within your photography that may have gone unnoticed.

A unique vision does not manifest overnight; it requires commitment, exploration, and honest reflection. As you forge your path, remember that artistry is not linear; it is a series of peaks and valleys—a dance with inspiration and frustration. It is essential to embrace imperfections and setbacks while celebrating small victories along the way.

As you cultivate your unique vision, consider the journey as an ongoing conversation between you and your art. The more you engage, the clearer your voice will become. Each click of the shutter not only captures a moment but also enriches your understanding of yourself and your perspective on the world. In doing so, photography transcends the act itself; it becomes a profound reflection of your identity.

In closing, I encourage you to take pride in your journey, trust in your vision, and remain curious. Explore the landscapes of your experiences and embrace all that makes you unique. The world of photography is vast and deeply personal, waiting for you to contribute your own chapter to its narrative. Embrace the beauty of seeing through your lens, for it is a gift that only you can share.

CHAPTER 9

TELLING STORIES THROUGH SERIES

The Power of Series

In the realm of photography, there is a transformative power that emerges when we shift our focus from isolated images to a cohesive collection—a series. A series of photographs can create a narrative that transcends the boundaries of a single frame, drawing viewers into a more profound and textured storytelling experience. Each image becomes a thread in a larger tapestry, weaving together emotions, contexts, and themes in a way that solitary photographs seldom achieve.

Reflecting on my own photographic journey, I recall the first time I explored the concept of photographic series. It was during a quiet summer spent in a small coastal town. The days were languid and unhurried, inviting me to stroll along shores that birthed both solitude and inspiration. I began to capture images that depicted the daily rhythm of life—the ebb and flow of the tides, the weathered hands of fishermen preparing their nets, and the vibrant colors of sunset blending seamlessly into the horizon. Initially, these images stood alone, each one a whisper of a moment. Yet, as I reviewed them, I noticed they began to converse with one another; they spoke of a common place, a shared experience, a season of life.

This initial collection became my first photographic series titled "Quiet Shores." I wasn't merely capturing the visual beauty of the location; I was tapping into a deeper essence that defined the spirit of that town and its people. Through the series, I sought to convey a sense of belonging, nostalgia, and the gentle rhythm of life that unfolded daily. The overarching theme of connection emerged clearly when reviewing the culmination of each image together; they told a more intricate story than any single photograph could encapsulate.

As you embark on your journey of creating a photographic series, it's essential to cultivate your vision. A series should begin with a theme that resonates with you—something you are passionate about. This theme serves as a guiding light, shaping the subjects you choose and the narratives you weave. It can be anything from the fleeting emotions of urban life to the stillness of nature, from cultural symbols to universal human experiences. Whatever your theme, allow it to speak to your heart.

Consider the famous series "The Americans" by Robert Frank, which captured the spirit of the U.S. in the mid-20th century. Each photograph is a story of its own, yet collectively they present a mosaic of American culture, illuminating aspects of society that were often overlooked. Frank's series encourages viewers to reflect critically on identity, belonging, and the intricacies of social life. His ability to create a cohesive narrative through a series of seemingly disparate images exemplifies the power held within a well-curated collection.

In creating a series, the process of discovery becomes as important as the end product. Take the time to explore your surroundings deeply. Spend hours observing a single theme until it reveals its complexities to you. As you delve into your subject matter, remain open to the stories that emerge. For instance, while photographing a vibrant local market, you may initially focus on the colors and textures of fruits and vegetables. However, over time, you might notice the interactions between sellers and buyers, the laughter shared, and the fleeting moments that tell a larger story about community and culture. Capture these nuances; they are what breathe life into your series.

The impact of a series often lies in its ability to evoke a sense of continuity and progression. A viewer journeying through a series experiences the same theme unfolding in various contexts—each photograph adding a layer to the narrative. Just as a well-structured story has a beginning, middle, and end, your series should have a rhythm that guides the viewer through a visual experience. Think about pacing; consider the emotional arc you wish to create. You might start with images that evoke curiosity, transitioning into those that evoke deeper emotions, and culminating with a resolution that leaves the audience pondering. The sequence of images can create suspense, anticipation, or even closure.

One poignant example resides in a series I created focusing on urban solitude titled "In the City, Alone." Initially inspired by the fast-paced, frenetic energy of city life, I began by photographing bustling streets and crowded cafes. However, as I delved deeper, I soon recognized that amidst the chaos, individuals often felt isolated, even surrounded by others. I focused on capturing those quiet moments of reflection—an individual lost in thought on a park bench, someone gazing out the window of a crowded subway, or a child playing alone in a background of vibrant city life. Each image highlighted the juxtaposition between the busy environment and the universal human experience of solitude.

Together, these photographs told a compelling narrative that people resonated with. They began to evoke empathy, inviting viewers to reflect on their experiences of loneliness and connection. When exhibited, viewers often remarked on how the series transported them into a shared emotional landscape, allowing them to recount their own stories, both personal and collective.

To encourage your own series creation, consider the following reflective prompts:

1. **Identify Your Theme**: What subject resonates with you? Are there specific themes you feel passionate about exploring through your lens? Consider cultural narratives, familial connections, ephemeral moments, or environmental change.

2. **Define Your Message**: What emotions or ideas do you wish to communicate? Avoid generic statements; think critically about the core narrative you want to convey through your series.

3. **Plan Your Shots**: Once you've identified a theme and message, sketch out potential images that could fit into your series. Aim for variety within your thematic structure.

4. **Capture the Unexpected**: Stay open to unplanned moments. Sometimes, the most striking images that define your series come from spontaneity.

5. **Reflect on the Sequence**: Once you've gathered a collection, begin to arrange your images thoughtfully. Consider how each photograph relates to your theme and the feelings you wish to evoke.

6. **Seek Feedback**: Share your work with trusted peers or mentors. Fresh perspectives can offer insights that enhance your understanding of how to mold and present your series.

As you work on your series, remember that storytelling in photography doesn't require perfection—it necessitates honesty, vulnerability, and connection. Embrace flaws, as they can often reveal personality and authenticity, allowing your series to resonate with viewers on a deeper emotional level.

Consider the celebrated series "Humanity" by photographer Steve McCurry. His images highlight the adversity faced by people across the globe, yet they also encapsulate moments of joy, resilience, and perseverance. Each image, albeit different in location and context, links back to a universal human experience, evoking a profound empathy and connection with the viewer.

It's also remarkable how series can allow for multi-dimensional narratives that can span time and space. Consider creating a project that evolves as your theme develops over weeks or months. Document changes in your subjects or environments. For instance, if your focus is on urban development, create a series capturing the same structure through various seasons or stages of construction. This approach not only highlights the passage of time but also symbolizes themes of change, growth, and transformation.

As you conceptualize and execute your series, allow yourself to be immersed in the process completely. Photography is not merely about the destination—it is about the journey. The stories you uncover, the people you meet, and the lessons you learn along the way will deeply enrich your work and enhance its authenticity.

Think of your series as a conversation with your viewer. Each photograph serves as a voice within this dialogue, inviting reflection and response. As you build your work, consider how your narrative might evoke varied interpretations and meanings. Diverse perspectives inherently exist within the realm of art—viewers will glean insights based on their experiences and emotions. Foster this dialogue and invite others to engage with the narrative you craft.

Ultimately, the power of series lies in its capacity to open gates to contemplation and connection. As you embark on your journey of storytelling through photography, remember to approach your series with intention and passion. Allow your images to speak stories that resonate with your viewers, fostering an emotional and profound connection. Through weaving together images, experiences, and emotions, you not only create art; you establish a bridge to understanding, empathy, and shared human experience.

As you conclude your series, take the time to reflect on the journey it has taken you on. What have you learned about your subject? What emotions or reactions emerged throughout your process? Celebrate the moments of joy and challenges faced—each has contributed significantly to your growth as a photographer and storyteller. Creating a cohesive narrative through a series of photographs is a captivating journey—one that reveals the intricate beauty of life and the power of visual storytelling.

As you prepare to share your series with the world, consider how you will curate and exhibit your work. Presentation can elevate your narrative, drawing viewers into the experience you've orchestrated. Think about how to display your photographs both physically and digitally to foster engagement and dialogue. Reflect also on the platforms you will use: will you follow traditional exhibition routes, or will you explore online sharing mediums that encourage conversation within digital communities?

In short, harness the power of a photographic series to amplify your voice and vision as an artist. Embrace the process, reflect on your growth, and foster connections. The stories you share through your work hold the potential to resonate profoundly, drawing others into the rich narrative threads that define our shared humanity.

Creating a Narrative Flow

Creating a cohesive narrative flow in a series of photographs is essential to transforming a collection of images into a compelling visual story. Each photograph, while it can stand on its own, is further enriched when it interacts with the images around it. This interaction creates not just a series of moments, but an unfolding narrative that draws the viewer into the story being told. In this exploration, we will dive deep into the concepts of pacing, sequencing, and image contribution, providing you not only with theoretical frameworks but also practical exercises that will encourage you to curate with intention and purpose.

To begin, let's consider what we mean by narrative flow in photography. At its core, narrative flow refers to the way the images relate to each other and how they guide the viewer through an emotional and thematic journey. This is similar to storytelling in literature or cinema, where the arrangement of scenes dictates the pacing and potential emotional response. The flow can be linear, where one image leads to the next in a straightforward manner, or it can be more abstract, allowing for nonlinear connections that evoke specific feelings or thoughts.

Understanding your key themes or messages is the first step in building a narrative flow. Identify what you want to convey through your series. It could be a personal experience, a social issue, or an exploration of a particular subject like nature, urban life, or human emotions. Once you have your central theme, it's easier to start thinking about how each photograph can contribute to the overall narrative. A clear thematic focus will guide your curating process, helping you to select and arrange images that reinforce the story you wish to tell.

Pacing is a critical element in narrative flow. It dictates the speed at which a viewer experiences the series. A slow pace might involve serene landscapes or intimate close-ups that invite contemplation, while a fast pace could be created using dynamic, action-oriented shots. Consider the emotional journey you want your audience to embark on; how do you want them to feel as they progress through your series? A well-considered pacing strategy aligns the viewer's emotional experience with the story's intent.

To illustrate the concept of pacing, let me share a personal experience. During a project focused on the quiet moments of everyday life, I curated a series that began in the early hours of the morning. The first few images depicted softly-lit scenes of a sleepy neighborhood, with gentle light filtering through windows and the quietness of streets just waking up. As the series progressed, photographs became progressively more dynamic as the day unfolded: children running to catch the bus, families gathering for afternoon picnics, and finally, the vibrancy of evening as people congregated in parks and cafes. The slow start mirrored the awakening of the day, while the rapid moments of interaction towards the end created a sense of energy and celebration. This controlled pacing engaged viewers, drawing them into the flow of daily life and encouraging them to appreciate both the quiet and lively moments.

Next, let's discuss sequencing. Sequencing is about the order of images and the relationship they form with each other. When images are sequenced thoughtfully, they can create tension, provoke thought, evoke nostalgia, or convey a sense of discovery. The goal here is to have each image serve as a stepping stone either toward a climax or resolution of the narrative. The sequence should not be haphazard; instead, it should reflect an intention, guiding the viewer seamlessly from one image to the next.

In my experience, I once worked on a series titled "Faces of Resilience," which showcased portraits of individuals who had overcome significant challenges in their lives. I began the series with wide shots that provided context about each subject's environment, immediately grounding viewers in their stories. As the series progressed, I transitioned to tighter portraits that capture the raw emotions and expressions of the individuals. This progression from context to intimate detail mirrored the journey from understanding to empathy, allowing viewers first to comprehend the larger narrative before diving deeper into the personal tales of resilience. The sequence of images acted as a direct invitation, encouraging viewers to connect emotionally with each subject's journey.

When considering your sequencing, think critically about the connections between images. Does one photo prompt a question that the next photo answers? Does an image create a stark contrast that highlights the theme? Aim to build layers of meaning as you sequence your photographs. You may pair contrasting images that resonate with the same feeling, or you might want to intersperse moments of tension with those of calm. These contrasts serve to enrich storytelling, revealing nuances that may otherwise go unnoticed.

Now that we have unpacked pacing and sequencing, let's focus on how each image contributes to the overall narrative. Each photograph should not just co-exist in the series; it should have a purpose. When curating your series, ask yourself: what role does this image play? Does it serve to develop the theme, escalate emotional tension, or provide relief? Each photograph should add value, either by deepening understanding or enhancing emotional resonance.

An effective exercise to guide this process is to create a storyboard of your photographic series. Using printed versions of your images, lay them out in a grid on a table or the floor. Observe how they interact and identify any images that seem out of place or disrupt the narrative flow. Rearranging the photos can help you visualize relationships and allow you to experiment with how different flow patterns change the story being told. This tactile approach can also provide fresh insights into your series and reveal images that may deserve more prominence.

As you engage in sequencing and discern the contributions of each image, don't shy away from instinct and emotion. Often, the most compelling narratives stem from a deeply personal connection to the subject matter being explored. Trust your gut feelings about how sequences resonate with you and your vision. Photography is not merely a technical exercise; it is about capturing the essence of experience and emotion.

To further enhance the narrative flow within your series, consider incorporating rhythm and contrast. A rhythm is developed through visual patterns or repetitions—like a particular color, shape, or theme that recurs throughout the series. This creates a visual heartbeat that can weave through the images, making them more cohesive and reinforcing the story's foundation. On the other hand, contrast injects energy into the flow. Opposing elements, whether it be light and shadow, color saturation, or content focus, stimulate interest and keep viewers engaged.

Once you have a clear idea of your pacing, sequencing, and image contributions, it's essential to detach and approach your series from a fresh perspective. Showing it to a trusted friend or fellow photographer can illuminate biases and blind spots you may have overlooked. Engaging with another perspective is invaluable; they may offer insights into the emotional flow and the clarity of your narrative that you cannot see alone.

As a practical exercise, consider creating a small series with a focused theme. Choose ten photographs that resonate with you, perhaps from recent outings or past work. After selecting these images, take the steps outlined previously. First, identify your core theme and the emotional thread that runs through your selected images. Next, arrange these photographs in several different sequences, taking note of how each arrangement influences the perceived narrative.

Reflect on the effectiveness of each sequence. Does the narrative feel compelling? Does one arrangement enhance what you hope to convey more than the others? This exercise not only hones your narrative skills but also strengthens your ability to see potential in the stories your photographs can tell.

In conclusion, creating a narrative flow in a series of photographs is a symbiotic interplay of pacing, sequencing, and intentional image contribution. By harnessing the elements of storytelling alongside thoughtful technical arrangements, you elevate a collection of photographs into a cohesive and evocative series. Allow your visions to translate into unmediated stories, drawing in your viewers through compelling narratives that speak to their experiences while engaging the heart and mind. Remember, take the time to experiment, refine, and, most importantly, trust your instincts as a photographer and storyteller. Your narrative awaits your discovery—take the journey!

Exhibiting Your Work

Exhibiting your work as a photographer is not merely about showcasing images; it is a profound act of sharing your vision, your experiences, and the narratives that resonate deeply within you. Whether you choose to display your photographs in a physical gallery or on an online platform, the experience of exhibiting your work can be transformative, both for you as an artist and for your audience. In this subchapter, we will delve into the importance of presenting photographic series to engage audiences effectively, share personal anecdotes from my exhibition journeys, and provide practical tips to help you prepare and succeed in your endeavors.

When I first began exhibiting my work, the idea seemed daunting. My early experiences were shaped by a mix of excitement and anxiety. One of my first exhibitions was a small pop-up gallery in my hometown, where I decided to present a series of black-and-white street photographs I'd taken over the course of a year. These images captured the essence of everyday life, revealing candid moments that spoke to the universal human experience. Standing in that room filled with strangers viewing my images felt both exhilarating and vulnerable.

It was then that I began to understand the true power of sharing my work.

Exhibiting photographs is not simply about displaying beautiful images; it involves telling a story that resonates with the viewer. Each series you create encapsulates a specific theme or narrative, and how you present that series contributes to the overall storytelling experience. When curating your exhibition, consider what emotions or thoughts you wish to evoke in your audience. Are you aiming to provoke thought, inspire nostalgia, or evoke empathy? The way you arrange your images, the lighting of the space, and the accompanying text can all influence how your work is perceived.

During one particular exhibition, I grouped my photographs based on specific emotions they conveyed. I created sections in the gallery dedicated to joy, melancholy, and introspection, allowing viewers to engage with the series more profoundly. As they moved from one segment to another, I observed how the flow of emotions transformed the experience. Visitors lingered in certain areas, sometimes sharing with me the memories my work had stirred within them. This feedback was invaluable, illustrating how a thoughtful presentation could enhance the connection between the audience and the photographs.

Physical exhibitions come with their own unique set of challenges and rewards. As you prepare to exhibit your work in a gallery, consider the space itself. Is it an intimate setting that enhances a more personal experience, or is it a large hall that demands bold visuals? Take time to visit the venue beforehand to understand its layout, lighting, and overall vibe. Is there a wall that stands out—a perfect backdrop for your series? Analyzing the venue will allow you to tailor your presentation accordingly.

I once exhibited a series in a spacious gallery with high ceilings and stark white walls. Initially, I thought that my intimate portraits would feel lost in such a vast space. However, by carefully selecting which images to feature and how to space them apart, I created a sense of conversation among the portraits. I positioned the images at eye level to invite viewers into the emotional landscape of each subject. This thoughtful arrangement not only made the work feel cohesive but also sparked discussions among visitors, who began to see the photographs as part of a collective human experience rather than isolated pieces.

Online exhibitions have gained popularity and have opened new doors for artists by reaching broader audiences. The rise of social media and platforms like Instagram, Artsy, and even personal websites has transformed the way we share our work. While an online exhibition might lack the tactile experience of a physical gallery, it offers unique opportunities for storytelling through interconnected images and captions.

For one of my online series, I embraced the notion of creating a visual journey. I organized my photographs into a digital format that allowed viewers to click through each image sequentially, telling a story that unfolded over time. Each caption provided context and insights into the emotions behind the photographs, allowing the audience to connect with the narrative on a deeper level. Leveraging online engagement tools such as Instagram Stories helped create anticipation among my followers, inviting them to participate in a live discussion on the themes presented.

Regardless of the medium in which you're exhibiting, one key element remains constant: presentation. Engaging your audience involves more than just hanging beautiful images or posting them online. To capture and hold attention, consider the following practical tips:

1. **Create a Cohesive Theme**: A well-defined theme helps to connect your series. It gives viewers a framework to understand your work and can enhance their experience. Select a guiding principle that ties your images together, whether it be emotional tones, colors, or subject matter.

2. **Tell a Story with Your Arrangement**: The way you arrange your images can influence the narrative flow of your exhibition. Think of how the order of images guides the viewer on a journey. Would a linear approach heighten the emotional

impact, or would a more abstract presentation encourage them to explore the connections between different images?

3. **Incorporate Textual Elements**: Captions, artist statements, and background information can enrich the viewer's experience. Providing context for specific images can spark curiosity and encourage a dialogue. Share insights into your creative process, the story behind the series, or even your emotional responses to the subjects.

4. **Involve Your Audience**: Interaction can deepen engagement. At a physical exhibition, consider hosting artist talks, discussions, or workshops where viewers can ask questions and share their thoughts. In an online space, encourage comments and discussions around the work. Responding to viewers can create a sense of community around your photography.

5. **Consider the Mixed Media**: In physical exhibitions, think beyond photography. Collaborate with other artists, include objects, or explore mixed media that can complement your series and make the exhibition more dynamic. In the online realm, consider integrating short videos, behind-the-scenes content, or audio that captures the surroundings while you were shooting.

6. **Promote Your Exhibition**: Whether in person or online, promotion is essential. Utilize social media, local press, and word of mouth to generate excitement. Leverage your networks to reach potential viewers, and don't shy away from partnering with local businesses, art organizations, or community centers to broaden your outreach.

7. **Prepare for Feedback**: Feedback from viewers can be invaluable. Be open to their interpretations and impressions; it can lead to unexpected insights and growth as an artist. Consider incorporating a feedback book or digital survey to gather thoughts from attendees about their experiences.

Engaging an audience is not a one-time interaction; rather, it's an ongoing relationship. After the exhibition, take time to reflect on the experiences you've shared, the dialogues that arose, and how your presentation influenced viewers' connections to your work. This reflection process is vital in understanding your artistic evolution.

I remember one series I exhibited based on the theme of "displacement," which resonated deeply with many attendees, some of whom shared their own stories of migration and belonging. After the exhibition, I received numerous messages from viewers, some expressing gratitude for highlighting a topic that felt intimate to them. This interaction clarified for me that as photographers, we are not just image makers—we are storytellers that can evoke emotional landscapes.

As you think about your journey with exhibiting photographic series, consider where you are now compared to when you first started. Perhaps your initial attempts felt clumsy or overly ambitious, but with each exhibition, you likely gleaned valuable lessons. This growth is something to celebrate and use as fuel for future endeavors.

Exhibiting your work is an opportunity to relish in the beauty of sharing your vision. It enables you to expose your inner world, the narratives you capture, and the emotions you wish to communicate. Whether you choose a physical gallery or an online platform—or perhaps a blend of both—remember that your goal is to engage, resonate, and connect with your audience. The act of exhibiting is, in essence, an invitation for dialogue, reflection, and deeper understanding—not just for those who view your photographs but for yourself as well.

In conclusion, the power of exhibiting photographic series lies in presenting work that engages and invites the audience to participate in the narrative. As you step into future exhibition opportunities, savor the connections you forge, the stories you share, and the changes that take place, not just for your viewers, but for you as an artist. Embrace each exhibition as a milestone in your journey, an avenue for growth, and an invitation to engage the world through your lens.

CHAPTER 10

THE FUTURE OF PHOTOGRAPHY

Emerging Technologies

As we step into a new era of photography, the impact of emerging technologies cannot be overstated. With advancements in artificial intelligence (AI), virtual reality (VR), and augmented reality (AR), the landscape of photography is rapidly transforming. These innovations not only redefine how we understand and create images but also alter the ways we engage with and experience visual storytelling. In this subchapter, we will explore these technologies, discussing their implications for photographers and the broader art form, accompanied by personal reflections and insights into how we can adapt to these changes.

AI has emerged as a powerful force in the creative industries, and photography is no exception. One of the most prominent applications of AI in photography is in the realm of image editing. Software powered by AI can analyze images, identify elements like faces, landscapes, and objects, and suggest enhancements or corrections. For instance, tools like Adobe Photoshop and Lightroom now incorporate AI features that can auto-enhance photographs, allowing photographers to achieve a polished look with minimal manual effort. While this efficiency can be a boon for busy photographers, it also raises questions about authenticity and the artistic process.

Reflecting on my own journey, I remember the hours spent in the darkroom during my formative years as a photographer. Each print was a labor of love, requiring patience and a deep understanding of the medium. With the rise of AI editing tools, I find myself grappling with the balance between embracing convenience and maintaining a personal touch in my work. I advocate for incorporating AI as a collaborator rather than a replacement for one's creative instincts. As we harness these technologies, we must retain the essence of our vision, using AI to enhance it rather than dictate it.

Another significant shift driven by AI is in the realm of content creation. Generative algorithms, a subset of AI, can now create highly realistic images from scratch. Imagine an algorithm trained on thousands of photographs generating an entirely new image that mimics the styles of professional photographers. This capability blurs the lines between human creativity and machine-generated art, prompting us to consider the nature of authorship in photography. As photographers, we need to define our role in this evolving landscape. Will we become curators of AI-generated content, or will we find ways to weave our unique perspectives into the fabric of technology-generated imagery?

Beyond AI, virtual reality is revolutionizing the way we experience photography. Traditionally, photographs have existed as static images confined to a frame or screen. VR takes this concept further, allowing immersive experiences that transport viewers into the scene. Imagine stepping into a 360-degree panorama of a bustling city street or a serene landscape, where you can absorb every detail as if you were physically present. This immersive approach opens up new avenues for storytelling, inviting viewers to engage with photography in a more visceral way.

I recall attending a VR photography exhibit where I was able to "walk" through a gallery filled with stunning landscapes captured by a talented photographer. Each scene enveloped me, allowing me to explore the nuances of the environment in a manner that a traditional photograph could not achieve. Such technology expands the potential for narrative depth, pushing us to think critically about how we can use VR to convey complex stories.

For photographers, adapting to VR means understanding not just the technical aspects of capturing 360-degree images, but also how to craft engaging narratives within this new medium. A powerful photograph can be experienced in moments, while an immersive VR experience requires a deeper investment of time and attention. The challenge lies in holding viewers' interest through evolving storytelling techniques, crafting a journey that resonates on multiple levels.

As we explore the intersection of photography and augmented reality, we see another dimension introduced to the art form. AR overlays digital information onto our real-world environment, creating a hybrid experience. Consider the potential for AR-driven photography exhibitions, where viewers can use their devices to interact with images in real-time. This interaction could include uncovering additional layers of information, such as behind-the-scenes stories or contextual details through a simple scan of a printed image.

While engaging with AR technology, I've often thought about how it can impact the viewer's experience. How will audiences engage with our work when they can personalize the narrative through their interactions? This dual-engagement creates a responsibility for photographers to consider the interpretive layer of their work. The complexity of the relationship between the viewer and the image is enriched as audiences navigate the interplay of reality and digital enhancement.

Amidst all this excitement, there are ethical considerations to keep in mind. As we incorporate these technologies into our work, we must also grapple with questions about privacy, consent, and representation. The advent of AI-generated images raises concerns about authenticity—what does it mean to capture a moment when that moment has been fabricated by an algorithm? In photography, we have historically been guided by ethical considerations around manipulation and representation. As we embrace new technologies, we must continue to reflect on how they affect our moral responsibilities.

The question of consent becomes essential in VR and AR as well. Photographers capturing real scenes may inadvertently infringe on the privacy of individuals who are not aware they are part of a panoramic photograph or an AR experience. Maintaining transparency and responsibly sourcing our narratives will be essential in this new frontier.

Moving forward, photographers must consider how to harness the power of these emerging technologies while ensuring authenticity in their work. The tools at our disposal are growing ever more advanced, presenting opportunities to expand our creativity but also demanding we remain vigilant about our artistic integrity.

As photographers navigate this rapidly changing landscape, I encourage readers to explore these emerging technologies through personal experimentation. Attend workshops that delve into VR and AR, play with AI editing software, and engage with other artists to share insights. Allow yourselves to be inspired by the frontiers of technology while remaining grounded in the human experience that defines our art.

The evolution of photography has always been marked by technological advancements—from the invention of the pinhole camera to the rise of digital photography. With AI, VR, and AR, we are experiencing another leap in this progression, one that invites us to rethink our roles as storytellers. Exploring these technologies grants us the power to create richer narratives and engage audiences on new levels.

In conclusion, the future of photography is intertwined with the advancements of emerging technologies. AI has the potential to enhance our creative processes, VR offers immersive storytelling experiences, and AR creates engaging interactions with our audience. As we embrace these changes, we must remain vigilant, thoughtful, and intentional about how we incorporate these tools into our work without sacrificing our artistic vision. The journey ahead is filled with potential—one that challenges us to adapt and redefine what it means to capture life's essence through the lens. The fusion of technology and photography offers an exciting horizon for exploration, one that I invite you to embrace wholeheartedly.

The Role of Photographers in Society

In today's rapidly changing world, the role of photographers has become increasingly complex and vital. As visual storytellers, photographers hold the power to document critical moments in time, shine a light on social issues, and inspire change through compelling imagery. This subchapter delves into the evolving responsibilities of photographers in society, examining how their work intersects with social justice, activism, and the broader narrative of human experience.

The power of photography lies in its ability to convey emotions and realities that may otherwise go unseen. Photographers are not merely technicians behind a camera; they are, in many ways, the historians of our time. As technology and society evolve, so too does the role of the photographer. The advent of digital media and social platforms has transformed not only how we share and consume images, but also the impact those images can have on society. With every shot taken, a photographer has the opportunity to capture more than just a moment—they can capture a message, a feeling, and, at times, a call to action.

Throughout history, photographers have used their craft to advocate for social change. A poignant example can be found in the work of photojournalists like Dorothea Lange, whose stark images of the Great Depression revealed the struggles of displaced families. Lange's photographs did more than document hardship; they ignited empathy and sparked a national response, leading to government initiatives that offered assistance to those in need. Her iconic image "Migrant Mother" is a testament to the power of visual storytelling—inviting viewers to connect with the shared humanity behind a deeply personal struggle.

As we navigate the complexities of the modern age, contemporary photographers continue to wield that same power. From humanitarian crises to environmental destruction, the lens becomes a tool for documenting injustice and engaging audiences with the emotional weight of photographs. Consider the work of photographers like Sebastião Salgado, whose documentary projects focus on social issues such as migration and deforestation. Through his black-and-white imagery, Salgado captures the intimate struggles of individuals while simultaneously shedding light on systemic global issues. His ability to evoke empathy through photography illustrates how images can transcend language and cultural barriers.

Reflecting upon my own experiences as a photographer, I am reminded of a project I undertook in response to a local community crisis. The area where I lived was experiencing a surge of homelessness, and I felt compelled to use my photography to capture the human side of this issue. Armed with my camera, I approached individuals living on the streets with the intent of sharing their stories. Each photograph became an invitation into their world—a visual narrative revealing not only their struggles but also their resilience and hope.

Engaging with these subjects required vulnerability and trust, both for myself and for those I photographed. I learned to listen deeply, to honor their narratives without sensationalizing their circumstances. Through this project, I was reminded of the ethical responsibility photographers carry when documenting human experiences, particularly those of marginalized communities. The challenge lies in balancing the need for advocacy with the dignity of the subjects being portrayed. My goal was to raise awareness while ensuring that the individuals I photographed felt empowered by their representation.

Furthermore, the intersection of photography and activism has seen an explosion of creativity and activism in the digital age. Social media platforms have democratized image sharing, allowing photographers around the globe to amplify their voices and engage audiences in urgent societal conversations. Hashtags like #BlackLivesMatter and #MeToo have mobilized millions, using the visual medium to spotlight systemic inequalities, raise awareness, and demand change. Photographers play a crucial role in curating these narratives, ensuring that they are seen and felt by audiences far and wide. The immediacy of digital photography allows for spontaneous documentation of events, which can serve as pivotal moments in an ongoing dialogue around social justice.

In this era, photographers are often at the frontlines, capturing moments of protest and resistance. Images from marches, sit-ins, and demonstrations tell powerful stories of courage and collective action.

These photographs serve as historical records, preserving the spirit of movements for future generations. Consider the iconic image of the 1963 March on Washington, where thousands gathered to advocate for civil rights. The photographs taken during that pivotal day not only encapsulated the crowd's determination but also reinforced the urgency of the fight for equality. Such images can motivate viewers to join movements, fostering a sense of connection and communal purpose.

To understand one's role as a photographer in society, it is essential that one reflects on the implications of their work. What narratives am I choosing to capture? Who has the power to tell these stories? How can I ensure that my photographic practice is rooted in ethical considerations? These questions encourage photographers to examine their motivations, perspectives, and the impact their images may have on their subjects and their communities.

As our discussion pivots towards personal reflection, I invite readers to consider their own roles as photographers in society. What stories do you feel compelled to tell? How can your unique perspective contribute to social dialogue? Engage with these reflective prompts:

- Identify a social issue or cause that resonates deeply with you. How could your photography shine a light on this issue? What approach might you take to ensure that your representation is respectful and authentic?

- Consider a moment in your life where you witnessed injustice or a significant societal issue. How might photographing that moment deepen the conversation surrounding the topic? Reflect on what you could capture that showcases the complexity of the experience.

- Think about the photographers you admire. What aspects of their work influence you? How can their approach to storytelling and social issues inspire you to reevaluate your own practices?

As you undertake your journey in photography, remember the capacity you hold as a visual storyteller. Your lens has the power to evoke empathy, provoke thought, and inspire action. Documenting the world around you is not merely about capturing beautiful images; it is about weaving narratives that resonate with truth and authenticity.

In navigating this responsibility, embrace the idea that photography can be a collaborative process. Engage with communities, listen to diverse voices, and allow your subjects to share their own stories. This inclusivity not only enriches your work but also honors the complexity and nuance of their experiences. Above all, keep in mind that the images captured through your lens can spark conversation, inspire movements, and create connections. By utilizing photography for advocacy and change, you become an integral part of a larger narrative—one that has the potential to shape perceptions, challenge injustice, and illuminate the human experience.

In closing, let us consider the role of photography within the context of our evolving society. It is not merely a medium for artistic expression, but a bridge to understanding the world's intricacies. Photographers are storytellers, advocates, and catalysts for change. As you forge your path in photography, remain steadfast in your commitment to use your skills to contribute to meaningful narratives that reflect the realities of our society. Your vision can illuminate the shadows of injustice, inspire hope, and foster empathy in an ever-demanding world. Embrace the power of your lens, and let your photography be a testament to the possibility of positive change.

As you venture forth, carry with you the knowledge that your role as a photographer is significant and profound; you have the capacity to shape discourse, influence hearts, and create impactful narratives that resonate across time and space.

Envisioning the Future

As I sit at my desk, surrounded by the lingering magic of countless photographs, both on paper and on my screen, I am reminded of my journey as a photographer. Each image tells a story, capturing moments that have shaped not only my craft but also my perspective on life. Photography has been more than just a passion or a profession; it has been a vessel through which I have explored the world, connecting with others and understanding the deeper nuances of humanity. Now, as we stand on the cusp of exciting technological advancements and cultural shifts in photography, it is time to envision our futures in this ever-evolving landscape.

What does the future hold for you as a photographer? This question invites reflection and introspection and invites us to recognize that our photographic journeys are uniquely our own. The world of photography is in constant flux. New technologies like artificial intelligence and mobile applications reshape the way we capture, edit, and share images. Social media platforms redefine the way we build communities, artistically collaborate, and engage with our audience. These changes present both challenges and opportunities, prompting you to consider how you can navigate the future and carve a path that aligns with your aspirations.

To help guide you on this journey, I would like to share my own aspirations and the vision I hold for my future in photography. Just a few years ago, I made a conscious decision to explore the intersection of storytelling and social impact. This intentional shift in focus has ignited a passion within me to use photography as a tool for advocacy and change. My aspiration is to create powerful visual narratives that speak to urgent social issues—stories that resonate deeply with viewers and compel them to take action.

As I reflect on my growth, I realize the importance of setting clear goals and intentions. The act of creating goals provides a roadmap, helping you measure progress while remaining flexible to adapt as new opportunities arise. Here are a few steps to consider when envisioning your future as a photographer.

Begin by identifying your core values and passions. What subjects inspire you? What stories are you eager to tell? Spend some time reflecting on these questions, as they will serve as the foundation for your photographic vision. For instance, if you are passionate about environmental protection, consider how you can incorporate that into your work. Could you explore themes of sustainability or create compelling images highlighting the beauty of nature?

Next, visualize your future. Close your eyes and imagine where you see yourself as a photographer five, ten, or even twenty years from now. What kinds of projects do you envision undertaking? Who do you see as your audience? Are you exhibiting your work in galleries, leading workshops, or perhaps collaborating with organizations that align with your values? Allow these thoughts to flow freely; use this visualization as a guiding star for your goals.

Once you have a grasp on your aspirations, it's time to set specific, measurable, achievable, relevant, and time-bound (SMART) goals. These goals will chart a course for your photographic journey, ensuring that you remain focused and driven. For example, if you aspire to exhibit your work, set a goal to submit your images to at least three galleries within the next year. If you want to explore a new technical skill, dedicate a specific amount of time each week to practice or take an online course.

To foster continuous growth and evolution, create a plan that allows you to regularly assess your goals and progress. Consider maintaining a photography journal, documenting not only your images but also your thoughts, reflections, and aspirations. By reflecting on your own images critically and honestly, you'll identify patterns in your work, discover areas for improvement, and celebrate milestones along the way. This practice of continuous self-assessment will keep your vision dynamic, enabling you to adapt as you grow.

Another crucial element of envisioning your future is recognizing the value of community and collaboration. Engaging with other photographers, mentors, and artists can inspire new ideas and perspectives, expanding your creative horizons. Seek out opportunities to connect with others who share your passions. Join local photography clubs, attend workshops, or participate in online forums. Collaboration can lead to unexpected outcomes, allowing you to push the boundaries of your creativity while fostering a supportive network.

In this digital age, leveraging social media and online platforms can also play an influential role in shaping your future. These platforms provide avenues for sharing your work and engaging with a wider audience. To build and nurture your online presence, consider creating an engaging portfolio website that showcases your strengths and unique style. Additionally, develop a consistent and authentic social media presence that aligns with your vision. Use these platforms not only to display your work but also to establish connections, seek feedback, and engage in dialogues with others.

While it's essential to remain open to the opportunities that technology brings, be mindful of the importance of staying true to your artistic vision. In a world inundated with images, discernment is key. Be selective about the projects you take on and the platforms you engage with. Make choices that align with your narrative and ethics. Your voice as a photographer is what will set you apart, and embodying your authentic vision will resonate with your audience.

As you navigate this journey, you will undoubtedly encounter challenges and setbacks. Embrace these moments as integral parts of your growth. Every obstacle you face provides invaluable lessons, offering insights into your resilience and expanding your capacity for creativity. Cultivate a mindset that welcomes these lessons, reminding yourself that the most significant growth often comes from the struggle.

Visualizing your future in photography is not just about the destination; it is about embracing the process. Each click of the shutter, each interaction with your subject, and each moment of inspiration contributes to your journey. Celebrate your steps forward, no matter how small, and allow yourself the grace to learn from missteps. The beauty of photography lies in its ability to capture fleeting moments, and the same applies to our own journeys.

Let's take this a step further with some practical exercises designed to help you envision and map out your future in photography. First, set aside dedicated time for creative brainstorming. Create a mind map or vision board that centers around your aspirations. Fill it with images, quotes, and ideas that inspire you. This visual representation of your goals will serve as a tangible reminder of the direction you wish to pursue.

Next, establish a timeline for your goals. Break down your overarching vision into manageable milestones, each with its own deadlines. Keep this timeline visible, allowing it to motivate you as you work toward your desired outcomes. Use a planner or digital app to track your progress and hold yourself accountable.

Consider launching a personal project that embodies your vision. This project can be an exploration of a theme you're passionate about or a series of portraits that capture the essence of your community. The important aspect is that this project aligns with your artistic identity and ignites your creativity. Dedicate consistent time to it and reflect on your progress throughout the process. Document your experiences, challenges, and triumphs in a dedicated project journal, serving as both a record of your growth and a source of inspiration.

Beyond individual projects, seek collaborative opportunities to broaden your experience. Approach photographers or artists whose work resonates with you, and propose a joint project or an exhibition. The synergy that arises from collaboration often leads to magnificent breakthroughs, offering fresh perspectives on both technique and vision.

Lastly, embrace the power of feedback. Share your work with trusted peers or mentors, inviting constructive criticism and insights. Consider joining critique groups or attending workshops to gain different viewpoints. The feedback received can spark deeper self-reflection and push you toward new goals, ensuring your artistic evolution remains vibrant and dynamic.

In closing, envisioning your future in photography is an empowering exercise that encourages you to take ownership of your creative journey. As you explore new opportunities and reflect upon your aspirations, remember that the path of a photographer is multifaceted and ever-evolving. By setting clear intentions and goals, nurturing your community, and remaining adaptable, you can navigate the exciting future that lies ahead.

The future of photography is not solely dictated by technological advancement; it is shaped by the stories we choose to tell, the moments we capture, and the connections we foster. You possess the unique ability to influence the world through your lens. Embrace the changes unfolding before you, taking risks and stepping out of your comfort zone. Let each photograph you capture become a testament to your journey, reflecting not just the world outside but also the world within. As you envision your future, trust in your instincts, remain curious, and pursue your vision with passion and purpose. The future is bright, and it is yours to capture.

—

CHAPTER 11

REFLECTIONS: YOUR PHOTOGRAPHIC JOURNEY

Assessing Your Growth

As you journey through photography, it's essential to take the time to assess your growth—the technical and creative evolution that shapes you as a photographer. Reflecting on your experiences not only allows you to recognize how far you've come but also identifies the areas where you wish to improve. In this subchapter, I invite you to embark on this introspective exploration, one that can deepen your understanding of who you are behind the lens.

Growth as a photographer is rarely linear. It often resembles a winding road filled with unexpected twists and turns. Much like the art itself, your journey is composed of many layers—technical skills, creative vision, emotional resonance, and personal stories. I remember standing in the midst of a bustling street festival a couple of years ago, camera in hand, feeling bewildered and excited. With every shutter click, I was absorbing moments: laughter shared between friends, a child reaching for a balloon, the golden glow of sunset reflecting off the rooftops. Those images were not just subjects; they were fragments of life that sparked my passion for storytelling through photography.

In that moment, I realized how much I had grown. My early days with an entry-level camera, which often resulted in poorly composed shots and missed focus, felt distant. I recalled late nights spent learning the intricacies of exposure, composition, and lighting, often feeling overwhelmed. Reflecting on that time brought me a sense of pride, reminding me that every struggle was a stepping stone toward the photographer I am today. Assessing your growth will not only instill this awareness but also motivate you to keep pushing your creative boundaries.

The importance of self-assessment in photography lies in its ability to carve a path for future growth. When you consciously reflect on your experiences, you can better understand your strengths and weaknesses. For instance, I've often found that my connection with subjects enhances when I approach photography with empathy, yet recognizing moments when I felt detached has guided me to focus on cultivating relationships with my subjects. This introspection is not about harsh self-criticism; rather, it's about finding a balanced view of your skills and desires.

To help you embark on this reflective journey, I've crafted a series of prompts that will guide your assessment. Allow them to inspire a deeper exploration of your photographic practices and philosophies. Find a quiet space where you can ponder and write down your thoughts; the act of writing can often lead to unexpected insights.

Begin with this question: What led you to photography? Recall the moments that sparked your interest. Was it the desire to capture beauty, express emotions, or tell stories? Reflecting on your initial motivation can reveal your passion's roots, highlighting how it has evolved over time.

Next, consider your growth in technical skills. Think back to your first camera. What were your primary challenges? Did you struggle with understanding exposure, composition, or post-production? Now, compare that with your abilities today. Can you confidently navigate the settings on your camera? Are you familiar with different lenses, and do you know how to use them for various effects? Write about the specific skills you've developed and any technical milestones significant to you.

As you assess your technical growth, don't forget to explore how your style has evolved. How has your aesthetic changed over the years? Consider the themes you gravitate toward now compared to when you first began. Do you notice a particular mood, color palette, or subject matter that resonates with you more?

Now turn your attention to creativity. Reflect on how your creative expression has blossomed through your journey. Take a moment to revisit the photographs that you consider your best work. What do they convey? How do they reflect your personal narrative or insights? What themes do you consistently explore in your photography? If you could define your voice as a photographer, how would you articulate it?

After contemplating your past and present, it's essential to examine your future. Where do you see yourself in the coming years? Consider the goals you want to accomplish. Write about the areas you wish to explore further. Perhaps there are styles or techniques you'd like to master or social issues you'd like to illuminate through your work. Setting clear intentions for your growth will provide a roadmap for your artistic journey ahead.

As you reflect, celebrate your achievements, no matter how small they may seem. Recognizing your progress fosters a sense of fulfillment that can fuel your passion. Look back at your portfolio or even revisit old folders on your computer. The photographs that once excited you may now feel outdated, but they are evidence of your evolution. Embrace those moments: the awkward framing, the harsh lighting, the missed opportunities—they are integral parts of your story.

Self-assessment is also an opportunity to identify the hurdles you've faced. What challenges have emerged along the way? Perhaps you've struggled with self-doubt or faced creative blocks. Reflecting on these obstacles offers valuable lessons. How did you overcome them? Did they lead to new discoveries or unexpected paths in your craft? Discussing challenges can deepen your appreciation for resilience— instead of viewing difficulties as setbacks, consider how they've enriched your journey.

Consider, too, the relationships you've built through photography. How have the connections you've formed shaped your perspective and practice? Has collaborating with other photographers, engaging with your community, or even interacting with your subjects influenced your work? Reflecting on the people who have impacted your journey highlights the importance of connection and collaboration in the photographic community.

As you conclude this introspective exploration, remember that growth is an ongoing process. Assessing your journey should not be a one-time event but rather a regular practice. With each new phase in your life, take a moment to reflect on your experiences, your aspirations, and your artistic vision. Embrace the ebb and flow of your creativity, understanding that every photograph you take contributes to your evolving narrative.

In sharing these reflections and prompts, my hope is that you feel inspired to embark on a journey of assessment in your photography. Each time you engage in this practice, may you find new insights, celebrate your achievements, and identify paths for further exploration. The journey of a photographer is not only about what you capture through the lens but also about what you learn along the way. Trust in your journey, and honor the growth that unfolds as you continually embrace the beauty of life through your art.

Setting Future Intentions

Setting intentions can serve as a compass for your photographic journey, guiding your creative decisions and providing clarity in times of uncertainty. Through my own experiences, I have come to appreciate the power of intention-setting and how it can illuminate the path ahead. As we embark on this exploration, I invite you to reflect deeply on what photography means to you, the stories you wish to tell, and how you envision your future as a creator of images. In this subchapter, we will delve into the significance of establishing clear intentions and provide practical exercises that will empower you to articulate your aspirations and form actionable steps toward achieving them.

When I first began my journey in photography, I navigated the creative landscape inspired by fleeting moments—the glimmer of light on a dewy leaf, the laughter of children playing in the park, or a fleeting glance of a stranger. Each moment compelled me to capture it through my lens, but it wasn't until later that I realized the importance of intention behind those captures. My early work was driven by spontaneity and curiosity, yet I often found myself overwhelmed by the abundance of choices and directions available to me. I was capturing fragments of life, but I lacked a clear vision of where I wanted my photography to lead me.

As I studied my body of work over the years, I recognized a pattern of growth. The more I set intentions for my projects, the more resonant and meaningful my images became. Setting intentions is a conscious act that allows you to define your artistic vision and creative direction. It can serve as a reminder of why you began this journey in the first place and keep you aligned with your core values and aspirations.

The first step in setting intentions is to engage in self-reflection. Take the time to contemplate your motivations for pursuing photography. What drew you to this art form? Is it the ability to tell stories, the joy of exploring new environments, the thrill of capturing transient beauty, or perhaps something more personal? Understanding your "why" is crucial, as it informs your creative approach and helps you uncover the themes that resonate with you.

I recall a pivotal moment in my journey when I sat down with a journal and reflected on my experiences behind the camera. I began writing about the images that had moved me the most and the stories that sparked my interest. I wrote about the emotions captured in a candid shot of an elderly couple holding hands and the raw energy displayed in a street photograph of a musician passionately playing their instrument. It became clear to me that I was drawn to moments of deep connection—whether between individuals or with their surroundings. This realization shaped my intention to focus on human stories in my future work, pushing me to explore more profound interactions within the context of my photography.

Once you have a clearer understanding of your motivations, it's time to articulate specific intentions for your photography. Consider drafting a personal mission statement that encapsulates your goals and values. This mission statement serves as a guiding light as you navigate your creative path. For example, mine might read: "I aspire to capture the essence of human connection through authentic moments that tell stories of love, hope, and resilience." By drafting this mission statement, I established a clear direction for my work, allowing me to filter the projects I took on and ensure they aligned with my vision.

As you develop your mission statement, think about the types of projects you wish to pursue. Do you envision creating a series of portraits that delve into the lives of your community, or perhaps documenting social issues that resonate deeply with you? The key here is to be specific—making your intentions as concrete as possible can empower you to take actionable steps toward achieving them. Instead of saying you want to improve your photography generally, consider specifics: "I want to create a body of work exploring the relationship between people and their environments, culminating in a gallery exhibition within the next two years."

With your intentions articulated, the next step is to break down those intentions into actionable goals. Setting measurable and achievable goals allows you to track your progress and make necessary adjustments along the way. Use the SMART

criteria—Specific, Measurable, Achievable, Relevant, Time-bound—as a framework for creating your goals. For instance, instead of merely stating, "I want to improve my technical skills," you could formulate a goal like: "I will complete an online photography course focused on advanced lighting techniques by the end of this month." This approach enables you to take tangible steps toward your aspirations, monitoring your progress as you go.

Moreover, consider the importance of timelines when setting your goals. Establishing a timeline creates a sense of urgency and accountability that can propel you forward. By determining deadlines for your projects or learning objectives, you create a framework that encourages you to stay committed to your intentions. Remind yourself that these timelines can be flexible. Goals may take longer than expected, and that's okay. The journey is rarely linear, and it's essential to remain adaptable as you pursue your passions.

In addition to setting your intentions and goals, it can be beneficial to cultivate a supportive environment that fosters your creativity. Surround yourself with like-minded individuals who share your enthusiasm for photography. Engage in conversations, share your intentions with fellow photographers, and seek feedback on your work. Community can serve as both inspiration and accountability—an invaluable resource as you navigate your photographic journey.

I remember attending a local photography meet-up where we discussed each other's intents and aspirations. Hearing others articulate their goals inspired me to refine my own practices and find ways to elevate my vision. There's something powerful about sharing your journey with others; it can ignite newfound energy toward your goals. Don't hesitate to find mentors who resonate with your artistic ethos or join workshops that expand your insights. Such relationships can catalyze growth, propelling you toward your intentions more seamlessly.

As you move forward in setting your intentions, remember to revisit them periodically. Your goals and aspirations may evolve as you gain new experiences and insights. Life is dynamic, and so should be your approach to photography. Allocate time to reflect on your progress, assess what has worked and what hasn't, and adjust your intentions accordingly. This practice of revisiting your goals will help ensure that you remain aligned with your passion and purpose.

To facilitate this reflective process, consider incorporating a regular practice of journaling or creating a vision board. Journaling about your experiences, emotions, and observations allows you to track your growth over time. It can also serve as a space to brainstorm new ideas and articulate them without fear of judgment. Meanwhile, a vision board can visually represent your aspirations and intentions, helping to clarify your artistic direction. Spend some time gathering images, quotes, or symbols that inspire you and arrange them in a way that resonates with your vision. Place it somewhere you can see daily—it will continuously remind you of what you aspire to achieve.

Practical exercises can help you deepen your connection to your intentions and refine your goals. Here are a few exercises to consider as you embark on this journey:

1. **Intention Mapping**: Grab a blank sheet of paper or a digital platform to create a mind map. In the center, write down "Photography Intentions" and branch out to explore various aspects of your practice—areas of focus, types of subjects, or themes that catch your interest. Allow your thoughts to flow freely during this activity; it may reveal new dimensions of your aspirations that you hadn't considered before.

2. **Goal Setting Workshops**: Find a quiet space to sit with your thoughts and take the time to draft a list of specific, measurable goals based on your photographic intentions. Categorize these goals into short-term, medium-term, and long-term objectives. Be as detailed as possible, specifying the steps you'll take to achieve each goal.

3. **Monthly Reviews**: Set aside time at the end of each month to review your progress. Reflect on what you accomplished, celebrate your successes, and identify any challenges you faced. Use this practice to recalibrate your goals and intentions if necessary, ensuring you remain on track as you continue your photographic journey.

4. **Dream Interviews**: Imagine your ideal future as a photographer—where are you? What are you shooting? Who are you sharing your work with? Write it out in an interview format, as if you're being interviewed about your achievements in five years. Consider the emotions you would feel discussing your success, the stories behind your images, and the impact of your work. This exercise can foster clarity around your

aspirations and embed them more deeply in your consciousness.

5. **Positive Affirmations**: Create a list of affirmations that reflect your intentions and goals. Write statements that encapsulate the confidence you have in your abilities. Examples might include, "I am dedicated to capturing authentic stories through my lens" or "I embrace the creative process with courage and curiosity." Repeat these affirmations regularly to reinforce your belief in your vision.

6. **Collaboration Projects**: Engage in collaborative projects that challenge you to step outside your comfort zone. Find a fellow photographer or artist and create a body of work together, operating with shared intentions. This exercise will not only expand your creative horizons but also provide fresh perspectives on your own intentions and how they can evolve through collaboration.

Remember, the journey of photography is as much about the process as it is about the final images. Setting intentions allows you to approach your work with purpose, creating a narrative that reflects your unique perspective as a photographer. Embrace the ebb and flow of your creative process, and trust in your ability to achieve your goals over time. Take pride in every step, from setting your intentions to capturing images that tell stories that resonate within you.

As you step forward into the future, allow your intentions to serve as a source of inspiration and grounding. Whether you find joy in exploring new subjects, experimenting with techniques, or connecting with others through your work, know that your journey is uniquely yours. Capture moments that resonate with your heart, share stories that matter to you, and let your passions breathe life into your photography.

Through intention-setting, you have the power to shape the trajectory of your photographic journey. As you bring your aspirations into focus, remember that each click of the shutter is an invitation to explore the world around you, to tell the stories that matter, and to document the beauty of life as it unfolds. Embrace this opportunity to craft a future steeped in creativity, authenticity, and purpose, and let your lens be a bridge to share your vision with the world.

Celebrating Your Journey

As a photographer reflecting on the countless moments captured and the lessons learned, it becomes clear that the journey is as significant as the destination. Each photograph holds a unique story, intertwined with triumphs and failures, each contributing to the tapestry of our personal and artistic growth. In this subchapter, I invite you to celebrate your journey, to reflect on the twists and turns that have shaped your perspective, and to recognize that every moment— whether seemingly insignificant or profoundly transformative—has played a pivotal role in who you are as a photographer today.

Many years ago, as I held my first camera, I remember the exhilaration swirling within me, a mix of excitement and apprehension. I had embarked on a path I had yet to fully understand, where I would slowly learn that a mere click of the shutter could encapsulate an emotion, a fleeting moment, a slice of life. I began in a small town where sunsets painted the sky with colors I had never seen before. On many evenings, I would wander, lost in the kaleidoscope of nature before me. It was during one of those twilight explorations that I took my first photograph that truly resonated with my heart. The hues of orange and lavender stretched across the sky, reflecting off a distant lake, the tranquility of the scene mirrored my inner calm.

But the journey was not without its hurdles. As my passion grew, so did my self-doubt. I remember a particularly crushing moment early in my career when I submitted my work to a local exhibition. After weeks of anticipation, the rejection letter arrived, each word cutting deeper than the last. In that moment, I felt the weight of every failed attempt and every "not good enough" echo in my mind. I questioned my vision, my skills, and whether I was cut out for this artistic pursuit. It took time and a willingness to confront these feelings that helped me understand that growth often comes hand-in-hand with setbacks.

Here lies one of the greatest secrets of photography: it's not merely about capturing moments; it's also about navigating through moments of vulnerability, disappointment, and resilience. Each photograph we take is a dialogue between ourselves and the world around us. The journey requires us to listen not only to our desire to create but also to where our heart is leading us. That rejection became a turning point; it pushed me to seek out constructive criticism and to invest more time in understanding my craft. With patience, I took steps toward improvement, turning pain into motivation. I learned not to view rejection as an endpoint but rather as a crucial part of the creative process.

Along the way, I found inspiration in the stories of others. I remember attending my first photography workshop, surrounded by fellow enthusiasts. We shared our experiences, our dreams, and our fears. Among the participants was a talented young woman named Maya, whose journey mirrored mine. She spoke of her struggle to capture her family's traditions, feeling torn between her artistic vision and her cultural obligations. Listening to her speak candidly about her challenges reminded me of the universal nature of our struggles as creators. In that roomfull of varying experiences and perspectives, I understood that everyone's journey is layered with both shadows and light.

As I immersed myself in different styles, experimentation became essential. There were countless evenings spent on the streets with my camera, engaging in street photography. With every click of the shutter, I learned to observe the world anew. I remember one encounter with an elderly man sitting on a park bench, his face crinkled with stories untold. I approached cautiously, striking up a conversation that revealed his profound love for his late wife and the memories that kept her spirit alive. Capturing that moment, I did not just take a photograph; I encapsulated a lifetime of emotions in a single frame.

Moments like this remind us that photography is not solely about technique; it's about connection. Celebrating your journey involves recognizing these connections, the relationships you build not just with your subjects but also with yourself. The more you connect, the more authentic your photography becomes. Each conversation you have as a photographer, whether brief or profound, adds richness to your narrative.

There was another time I stepped out of my comfort zone. I wanted to document a local festival that celebrated diversity and community. Initially, I felt apprehensive; the thought of intruding on people's happiness made me uneasy. However, after striking up conversations with locals and immersing myself in the vibrant atmosphere of the event, my lens transformed from an outsider's view into an empathetic participant. The images I captured celebrated joyful moments—laughter, dance, and connection—that I had never anticipated. In sharing those images, I began to understand the power of storytelling through visuals.

Our journeys are also marked by laughter, joy, and unexpected serendipities. I vividly recall a trip to a coastal town where I intended to photograph the sunrise. Waking up early, I stumbled upon a small café where locals gathered for coffee. It was a spontaneous decision to set my camera down and join them. The conversations flowed, and the warmth of human connection invigorated me. Later, as I captured the sunrise, the joy of that morning was infused in every shot.

These moments remind us that life is not confined to our lenses; it unfolds in the spaces we allow ourselves to engage in.

Your photographic journey is also about how you navigate through life itself, discovering beauty, kindness, and moments of connection.

In essence, it's crucial to celebrate your growth, your failures, your triumphs, and the reflections you have gained. Each phase of your journey deserves acknowledgment. Consider dedicating time to revisit your early photographs. Reflect upon your technique, your vision, and the emotions you felt when you clicked that shutter. Recognize how you've matured and evolved, refining your perspective and understanding of your craft.

Moreover, you may consider documenting your journey through writing or journaling. Capture your feelings about particular photographs, the challenges you faced, and what inspired you throughout your growth. This will not only serve as a powerful reminder of your resilience but also as a source of inspiration when you hit creative slumps in the future. Think of it as creating a roadmap that over time will highlight your evolution and the unique signature you bring to the world of photography.

As you celebrate your journey, remember to embrace vulnerability. Each struggle, each failure, each success is inherently tied to your unique narrative. Acknowledge that, like the seasons, your journey will fluctuate. There will be moments of flourishing followed by times of introspection. Allow yourself to rest during these phases, knowing that creativity ebbs and flows.

Take a moment now to appreciate those who have influenced your path. Reflect upon mentors, peers, and even strangers whose stories intertwined with your own. Let gratitude accompany your gaze as you flip through the memories you've captured. Your lens has the power to reveal stories that echo through generations, stories filled with trials, happiness, nostalgia, and hope.

Photography has the capacity to immortalize those fleeting moments, but it also offers us the ability to weave our narrative into the larger tale of humanity. As you continue to pursue this art, remain steadfast in the knowledge that every photograph tells a story, a sliver of existence frozen in time.

To celebrate your journey means to embrace the artistic spirit with enthusiasm, passion, and dedication. It is about remaining curious, continually learning, and welcoming new experiences. Allow your love for photography to be both the light that guides you and the fire that fuels your creativity.

As we conclude this exploration of your photographic journey, I encourage you to take the next step with confidence. Seek out that next project that excites you, plunging into the unknown with the knowledge that growth comes only when we push ourselves beyond our limits. Capture narratives that resonate, whether they involve strangers on the streets, a close friend's laughter, or the beauty of a petal blooming in a garden.

In this ever-evolving journey of self-discovery, hold tightly to the stories that have shaped you and project them into the world with unabashed authenticity. Your voice matters; it is an integral part of the collective story we create as artists in a shared universe.

As you move forward, take time to reflect, to celebrate, and to encourage others in their journeys. Share your triumphs and your failures, your insights and your discoveries. Build a community rooted in support, knowing that every voice adds richness to the narrative we craft in photography.

Embrace the fullness of your journey, for it is an ongoing exploration filled with beauty, complexity, and limitless potential. Your lens captures more than mere images; it captures the essence of existence itself. Each click carries the weight of your experiences, and in doing so, you celebrate not just photography, but life itself. Let your vision evolve, let each moment inspire you to explore further, and as you do, celebrate the unique journey that is yours alone.

CONCLUDING:

THANK YOU FOR JOINING THIS ADVENTURE!

As we wrap up this journey, I want to take a moment to genuinely thank you for investing your time and energy in exploring the craft of photography with me. Together, we've navigated through the intricacies of the art form, from understanding the emotional bonds that grant depth to your images, to harnessing the unstoppable power of light and composition. Always remember, photography is not merely a technical skill; it's an expressive outlet that can stir emotions and tell powerful stories. I hope that by now, you've collected more than just knowledge; I hope you've harvested your own enthusiasm, creativity, and boundless inspiration!

Many of the lessons we've discussed were underpinned by personal experiences that shaped my own path as a photographer. I shared them not just to illustrate points but to encourage you to reflect deeply on your creative journey. Every chapter was packed with practical exercises and prompts designed to help you push past your comfort zone and embrace your unique vision. Whether you tried something completely out of left field or revisited your old favorites with a new perspective, I commend you for taking those brave steps!

Your growth as a photographer is not a destination but rather a thrilling expedition. The magic lies in embracing the entire process

— the mistakes, the triumphs, and every composition in between. So, revisit those pages whenever you need a spark, and don't hesitate to pick up your camera and venture outside. The world is brimming with stories just waiting for you to capture them. Remember, every photograph has the potential to convey profound emotions, even the simplest snapshot can tell a story!

As you carry these lessons forward, think of photography as a lifelong companion. Keep experimenting, exploring, and connecting with the world around you. The beauty of this craft is that it evolves with you — there are no limits, no barriers, just endless opportunities to grow. Whether you're aiming to become the next groundbreaking photographer or just capturing everyday moments, let your heart guide you to see the extraordinary in the ordinary.

Lastly, as I close this chapter of our shared adventure, I invite you to keep the spirit of creativity alive in your daily life. Keep seeking inspiration, reminding yourself that the joy of photography lies in connection, storytelling, and a deeper appreciation of the world. Thank you for being a part of this journey, and I look forward to seeing what unique story you'll tell next through your lens. Now, go out there and create magic!

With immense gratitude and enthusiasm,

Bernard